CW00338935

THIS PRIZE IS DANGEROUS

Who killed Freddie Sanchez, Quin Jefferson and
Silas Griffin?

Join Matthew Prize, ace detective, professor of
criminology and chocolate addict as he tracks down the
secrets of the wealthy residents of sunny California to solve
a puzzling series of murders.

And for one lucky reader who successfully exposes the
murderer, there is a special reward

THIS PRIZE IS
DANGEROUS

Matthew Prize
with
Otto Penzler

A STAR BOOK

published by
the Paperback Division of
W.H. Allen & Co. PLC

A Star Book
Published in 1985
by the Paperback Division of
W.H. Allen & Co. PLC
44 Hill Street, London W1X 8LB

Copyright © 1985 by Whodunit, Inc.

Phototypeset in Linotron Plantin 11/12pt
by Input Typesetting Ltd, London
Printed in Great Britain by
Anchor Brendon Ltd, Tiptree, Essex

ISBN 0 352 31724 8

CONTEST RULES
A
REWARD

if you can solve the mystery in
THIS PRIZE IS DANGEROUS
A Whodunnit Mystery

THE PRIZE

1. There is one prize of £1000 on offer to entrants from the UK, Canada, South Africa and Europe, and another prize of Aust. $1500 on offer to entrants from Australia, New Zealand and the Far East.
2. No substitution or transfer of prize is permitted.
3. Taxes on prize money are the winner's responsibility.

HOW TO ENTER

1. Complete the Official Entry Form on page 7. You may submit as many entries as you wish for either of the two cash prizes, but not both, and all entries must be submitted on an Official Entry Form. Answers submitted without an Entry Form, or with any part of the Entry Form incomplete, are automatically disqualified. The Official Entry Form may not be copied or reproduced. Competitors who enter for both cash prizes will also be disqualified.
2. Each separate Entry Form must be accompanied by a processing fee of 50 pence sterling, or equivalent as of 19 September 1985, if entering for £1000 prize, or Aust. 50 cents, or equivalent as of 19 September 1985, if entering for Aust. $1500 prize. Payment must be by cheque, money order or postal order only.
3. Send Entry Form and processing fee to THIS PRIZE IS DANGEROUS COMPETITION, W H Allen & Co PLC, 44 Hill Street, London W1X 8LB for £1000 prize, or THIS PRIZE IS DANGEROUS COMPETITION, Gordon & Gotch Ltd, 114 William Street, Melbourne, Australia 3000 for Aust. $1500

prize. Entries should arrive no later than 15 January 1986. No Entries received after that date will be considered. Proof of posting cannot be accepted as proof of delivery, and no responsibility can be accepted for entries lost, delayed or damaged, before or after delivery. Entries are the property of W H Allen & Co PLC and will not be returned.

4. All cheques or money orders or postal orders should be made payable to W H Allen & Co PLC for £1000 prize competition, and to Gordon & Gotch Ltd for Aust. $1500 competition prize. No other means of payment will be accepted. Any other means of payment, or non-payment of the entry fee, will result in disqualification.

5. This competition is open to anyone aged 16 and over, except for employees of W H Allen & Co PLC and their families. The contest is void wherever prohibited or restricted by law.

JUDGING

1. The correct answers as determined by the authors are based on clues found in the book.

2. All entries will be judged by the Managing Director of W H Allen, the Editor of Star Books and well-known author Peter Haining.

3. If more than one entry (or no entry) has the correct answers to all the questions, the winner of the competition will be the entrant who, in the opinion of the judges, best answers the tie-break question. The decision of the judges will be final. No correspondence will be entered into, acknowledged or returned. Details of the results of the tie-break question will not be disclosed.

4. The winner of the competition will be notified by post on or before 14 February 1986. The winner and winning solution will be announced on 28 February 1986 in *The Times* of London, *The International Herald Tribune* (European Edition), *The Listener* of New Zealand, *The Australian*, and *The Cape Town Times*.

Chapter One

I was sitting in my cluttered little office contemplating the work of Emile Durkheim, as well as the disc of sunshine floating on the crisp blue ocean beyond my window and down the mountainside. Durkheim was part and parcel of the Associate Professorship in Criminology dodge I was currently trying to cope with and the view of the Pacific came with every office in the Brewer Sociology Building at Cal State San Amaro. It was midafternoon, the sun had hooked up over the coastal mountain range and begun its descent toward Hawaii and points west, and Durkheim, as well as the slab of Hershey bar I'd just polished off, was working the old familiar magic. I was half-asleep.

The knock at the door had grown pretty insistent by the time I'd struggled back to Planet Earth and figured out where the hell I was. I cleared my throat, noisily slammed the book shut and told my visitor to come on in.

She was wearing a tee-shirt which I read as she came toward me.

> *Melanie*
>   *If I can't find a dress for the party*
> *by tonight . . .*
>   *It's curtains!*
>   *Scarlett*

Like a fool I tried to avoid staring at her nipples. I wasn't up to the challenge as it turned out. Finally I just gave into it. Made me feel young again.

'Oh, Doctor Prize,' she sighed, dropping a Yo-Yo Ma carry-all next to the ratty old easy chair I sometimes read in, 'thank God you're here. I was afraid . . .' She was a small and very perky blonde from one of my classes. Criminology One. Always took notes, had done well on the quizzes. She'd hung around after class a couple of times to ask questions and she'd gone out of her way to chat me up once in the college Rathskeller where you drank beer from plastic mugs that almost looked like glass from about ten feet away. She'd made eye contact and I'd gotten the impression that there was a brain between her two small delicate ears. What might be percolating in the brain was something else, well beyond my commission as associate prof. Her name was Sue Griffin. For some reason, in the privacy of my smutty fantasies, I thought of her as Susie.

'I'm not a doctor,' I said. They never learn.

'Okay, okay, Professor Prize, then – '

'I'm not a professor. I'm more of an academic third-base coach, get it?'

'No. But – ' She bit a thumbnail. Fortunately it was her own. 'But . . . I really need to talk to you. You're the only person I know who might – oh, I don't know.' She slumped back in the chair. I prayed that there were no personal problems on her agenda. Then I prayed that her nipples would get soft and sort of go away. Of course I was denied both requests.

'Tell me, Miss Griffin, what do you make of your tee-shirt? Have you in fact read it? Or are you waiting for the movie?'

'What are you talking about?' She pushed her chin

10

back and frowned, peering down at the legend punctuated by the erectile tissue. 'What movie?'

'*Gone With the Wind*. Have you read it? Or seen it?'

She shook her head. 'I'm not big on movies – '

'Then what do you make of your tee-shirt?'

'I don't make anything of it. This TA in the film department gave it to me. Got me to go to *Blood Beach Revisited* and *Hell Motel: The Second Night* and he gave me the shirt, okay? It doesn't mean anything to me – look, I want to talk to you about something real personal, okay? So could we drop the movie rap?'

I shut my eyes and I'm afraid I groaned.

'Are you okay?'

I nodded. 'One too many enchiladas. It's nothing. Are you sure you want to talk about any personal matters with me? I mean, would you be more comfortable with your advisor or one of the counsellors?'

'No, you're the perfect person. It's just that I haven't known if I should talk to anybody. But I guess I'd better 'cause I keep worrying – '

'Why me? I'm selfish and not very sympathetic – '

'Oh, that's okay. I'm the same way.' She pushed a grin slowly out of the corner of her mouth. 'The thing is, you're the only detective I know.'

Oh, shit. I should have thrown her right out of my office then and there. Having a well-developed death wish, I leaned back, looked into her Baby Blues and those big white Ultra Brites, and figured it couldn't hurt just to listen.

It was damn near Curtains, Melanie.

It was her father. He was lost and she was looking for him. I felt like I could feel the outline of a sort of assbackwards Ross Macdonald novel. Lew Archer had always made me feel very guilty for being kind of a smartass myself. I read those books and looked at my silly little career in skip-traces and wandering husbands or wives and kids who went off to join the Moonies for a summer and wound up bugging truculent tourists in airports – I thought about my career and toughed it out with Lew who was always up to his neck in the most eternal of the verities, and I'd feel guilty as hell for being a happy guy. Obviously I was missing the point. Maybe Susie Griffin would show me the light. Maybe she had stepped out of Lew Archer's filing cabinet to lay some meaningful sorrow on old Prize. I asked her to tell me about her father. Starting with his name.

She took a deep breath and made heavy work of organizing her thoughts. It always worked, though: ask them to start with the name and give you a kind of thumbnail bio. Calms people down, makes them think methodically.

'Silas Griffin,' she said. 'That's my dad. He's fifty or so. Very smart, sort of a genius in his own way. If he were a kid he'd be the most dangerous kind of computer hacker, probably getting himself arrested. Curious, he's so curious about things. And he tinkers. Or he did – but he's gone!'

'Whoops,' I said. 'We'll get to that. First, what does he do? For a living, I mean – '

'Oh, well like I said – computers. It's just that he's not a kid. He's an inventor and a designer. Designs computer programs, the software. But I'm not into computers, y'know? Probably childish rebellion but what can I do about it? We always had computers around the house, in the basement, the garage, the dining room. I'd just as soon never see another one – I hate 'em. They symbolise the whole loss of privacy, the final victory of control, Big Brother . . .' She suddenly stopped, as if she'd been on that tangent

12

enough times to know that it wasn't all that original and therefore wore thin pretty quickly.

'We? Who is we?'

'Well, you know, the family . . . dad and mom and my brother and me. Look, I think we're wasting time, Professor. This is about my dad. Not about them. I mean, he and mom are divorced and she wouldn't know what I'm so worried about – '

'Fine. Now let's get to the part where he disappears. When and from where?'

'Well, he's been missing for . . . for . . .' She went after that little thumbnail again, gnawing. I saw the point of her pink tongue peek out. She was probably twenty-one. Let's see. I was thirty-three or forty-three or fifty-three. Something with a three in it, anyway. Was she within my first strike capability? Or out of range? Idiotic train of thought. I hoped she wasn't going to cry. She bit her lip. There was precious little left to chew on. That she could reach, anyway.

She swallowed away the inclination to drizzle a tear. Game girl. 'I feel so awful, he's been missing for weeks and weeks . . . and I haven't done a thing about it until now. Such a rotten daughter. And I *care*, I really do care about him – '

'Don't be too hard on yourself,' I said. I opened my desk drawer and brought out a sack. 'M & M?' She shook her head. I counted out four and scarfed them down, put the sack away and shut the drawer. Dirty little addiction. 'Children are not as a rule responsible for their parents. Parents worry about children who wander off. Children seldom notice the same behaviour in their parents. So, Dad's leading his own life – maybe he just took a trip. Maybe he won a prize, round the world tour – I take it you just don't know. Where was he the last time you knew?'

'For the past year he's lived aboard his yacht, the

13

Baja Dream. Fifty-five footer.' She stood up and went
to my window. There was a stack of *Penthouses* on the
bookcase running beneath the glass. She leaned on
them, craned forward. 'No,' she said, shaking her
head. 'I thought maybe you could see it from here.
It's in the San Amaro Marina but it's too far off to
the left, the south. You know the Marina, though?' I
nodded. I made a fool of myself at boat parties as
often as the next man. If the next man was Huntz
Hall.

She talked a bit more about the disappearance,
nothing substantive, and then she ran out of gas. I
said: 'Look, let's get serious about this, Miss
Griffin – '

'Please, call me Sue.'

'How about Susie?'

'Ick. I hate that – '

'Fine. Susie, it is. Have you notified the police?
That's sort of standard in things like this – '

She shook her head. Determinedly. 'Mother says
he's probably just off getting polluted – that's her
word, it would be – and he'll turn up and then if I've
made a big deal out of it I'll feel like an idiot. Mother
is pretty adept at making me feel like an idiot. She
says he's off somewhere, Mexico, Cancun or some
place, and I'm being an alarmist . . . and there's no
one else but me to care about him!' The tear finally
escaped but she didn't make a big deal of it. She
brushed it away with her hand, like a little girl. 'My
brother hasn't even spoken to him since the divorce.
That's the kind of family we are, I guess. Not much
of a recommendation – '

'Maybe not. But,' I said brightly, 'very modern. A
cross section of the American family. Beautiful girl,
bitter mommie, boozed-up daddy, and snotty son.
Just be glad you're the beautiful daughter – '

14

'You're very nice,' she said and started choking back some more tears. 'Damn,' she muttered, prying her eyelid open. 'You start wimping around like I'm doing now and your contacts float away. Damn.' I looked away from the little paroxysm of intimacy, grabbed a handful of Kleenex and dropped them in her lap. She said something and began dabbing her cheek.

'What about your father's job? Isn't his employer bound to be concerned?'

'Oh, he doesn't *work* for anyone.' Now her nose sounded all stuffed up. 'I guess I'm not giving you a very good picture of him. He's a heavy hitter, y'know? Inventor. Entrepreneur. Fifty-five foot yachts aren't exactly chopped liver. He makes his designs and sells them on a freelance basis, mainly to firms up in Silicon Valley. He used to be just about the king of the video game designers. All the bip, bong, zap, rattle, crash sounds you hear coming from the arcades when you walk past? Or down in the Student Centre? That's my dad. But that was just a phase. Lots of money but he got bored after a while. The last thing I heard about was a series of programs for a hot new line of pc's – that's personal computers, y'know – '

'However strange I may look to you, Susie, I have been a resident in good standing of Earth for several years now. I know what a pc is – '

'I just meant to excuse myself for using jargon. I hate jargon. You never use it in class – '

'Only because I don't actually know it yet. However. Back to Dad. Yes, I can imagine the kind of money he must have been making. Tons.'

She nodded. 'These companies, with their stock going crazy, jumping up and down with each rumour, they loved to announce that Silas Griffin was coming on board with some new gizmo – and of course he's

15

only human. He loved it. The excitement, the ego massage, the money . . . I've got to admit that when he'd pull off some big deal, sign some big contract, get a huge royalty cheque – well, he had a lost weekend from time to time. Bottom line, his drinking habits went a long way toward causing the divorce. Driving the wedge between them. I guess nothing but the personalities scraping against each other ever causes the divorce . . . but the drinking was a factor. Or one of mom's excuses. I don't know. It gets pretty confused whenever I try to figure it all out – '

'Yeah, well, I'm sure it's just as confused for your mom and dad when they try to get it all clear in their minds. That's just the way those things are.'

She nodded and I almost reached across and squeezed her hand, which probably would have broken some ancient blue law and kept me out of the godawful mess I got into. But I didn't. I thought about the M & Ms in the drawer. Then I said: 'Well, if you don't want to take all this to the cops just yet . . . look, what you need is a private detective. He could ask a few questions, follow up a lead or two, find your daddy drying out in a motel somewhere and put life back together for the Griffins.'

She looked at me like I was two bricks short of a load.

'But you *are* a detective, Professor – '

'Call me Matt.'

'You *are* a detective, Matt. That's the whole point.'

'That was a long time ago,' I said.

'What do you mean? How old are you?'

'Who the hell cares? It's got a three in it, okay? And I feel older than I am. You know why? The private eye scam, that's why. It ages a man. Look at Lew Archer . . . look at Nick Charles, a lush! You worry about some weird guy who doesn't want to give

16

you back the keys to the car but doesn't want to make the payments either, you worry about a guy like that shooting your face off – and it ages you. That's why I got out. Mug's game – '

'You mean you just chickened out?'

'Right on,' I said.

'You sound like Jim Rockford! Are you doing that on purpose?'

'Jim who? Look, I was a spectacularly unsuccessful private eye. I even got shot once. I couldn't shoot back because I forgot to put the bullets in my gun. I had to play dead. Can you believe that? So, naturally I was the perfect choice to teach criminology . . .'

'Gosh,' she said, regarding me in a new light. 'I don't know what to say – '

'If you had a grain of human decency, you'd could tell me I'm being too hard on myself.'

She laughed. 'I knew you were just kidding!'

I nodded shyly, the campus moron.

'You'll help me, then? I just know something's happened to him, Matt. I'd do it myself – I mean, I've learned a lot in your course, but – you know how it is – I don't feel I'm quite up to investigating it on my own.' She was serious, God love her. How could I tell her that my description of my performance as Don Quixote-the-detective was right on the money.

'That's wise, you're not quite a licensed operative yet.' I still had my licence. I still had my gun. I still had a tight grin, a roll of quarters to use in my fist, and boyish charm that knew no bounds. 'But maybe your mother really knows her man. Maybe he's just sailed down to Mexico with some ladies – '

'I think that bothered mom, too. Though you'd never know it now. Whew.'

I let all that whistle past my ear like a stray slug. I

17

didn't have the top of one ear, actually, due to such a slug that didn't quite manage to whistle past.

'But,' she said, 'he didn't just go sailing off to anywhere. His boat's still at the marina. I have a key to it. But he's not on board. There's no sign of him. There's no sign of anything unusual – it's like Sherlock Holmes's dog in the night.'

'The one that didn't bark,' I said.

'Exactly. There's no sign of anything unusual on the boat. Which is absolutely unusual – in residence, my father keeps the messiest boat in the world.'

She gave up on the contacts and I had to look away while she stuck her finger into first one eye and then the other, bringing them out and depositing them into the little dual-celled plastic container. She breathed a sigh of relief. She fumbled around in the Yo-Yo Ma bag. There was a depiction of a cellist on the dark green canvas. The kids, I thought, are gonna be all right. Then she put a pair of round, wire-rimmed glasses on her short, tilted nose, and smiled to tell me she was ready to push on.

'Tell you what I'll do,' I said, acting like Rockford. I was just kidding her. I loved Jim Rockford, never missed the re-runs. That's what VCRs are all about. Listen, I'm technologically hip, man. 'Let's go talk to your mother and get a reading on what she thinks. Maybe she'll be a bit more forthcoming with me. And then, who knows? Maybe we'll take a look at the boat. Can't hurt. And if I find anything that looks suspicious, I'll get some of my friends on the police force to go to work on it.'

'I don't see any point in going back to the boat,' she said. 'We'd just be wasting time if something has happened to my father.'

'Who would want to harm him, Susie?' I was trying

18

to find my keys and grab my blazer and leave the desk in some order.

'Somebody in the computer business – all I can think about is how cutthroat it is. Maybe somebody from overseas. I mean, everybody's in that business now. That rat race. It's like the space race and the missile race . . . so much money involved. Doing something to Silas Griffin wouldn't make any difference to some of those people – they'll do anything . . .'

I took her elbow and steered her out the door. 'Let's not worry about that until we have to. For now, let's go see your mother.'

I felt her shrink away. I wrote that off to mothers-and-daughters.

Chapter Two

San Amaro was curled around the big bay like a fat and flakey croissant, the hills rising gently from the sparkling blueness of the ocean, all stucco and tiled roofs and thick green foliage, bright shellbursts of flowers. Money, by and large, can buy pretty and there was a hell of a lot of money in San Amaro. So it was very pretty. We drove in our own cars, me tight behind her. She drove a little gold Mercedes. One tail-light was shattered. No big deal. About four hundred bucks. I was bounding along in my little red VW ragtop. It was fifteen years old. I'd once been married to a lady who wrecked that little red VW not once, but twice. Consequently it was what I got – salvaged – from the divorce. She'd driven it directly into the side of a Land Rover the last time. The Great White Hunter had leaped from the dust, straightened his custom made safari jacket, and caught sight of the culprit. His anger turned to goodnatured cajolery and Greta married him six months later. They went to Africa on their honeymoon and so far as I know were never seen again. More power to them. The windshield was still cracked where her head had hit it. Everytime I saw the crack I thought of her and smiled. Sentimental son of a gun.

We wound up through the hills, passed on through a wrought iron gate in the shape of two palm trees reaching for each other, and past a man-made lake with a fountain jetting up in the centre, like Griffin's own personal Old Faithful. Eventually the house came into view, your standard two-decker Spanish job with dark wooden balcony, hanging baskets of scarlet flowers that looked like exotic candy, a couple of Japanese gardeners squirting hoses at each other, three more Mercedes strewn around the forecourt. Nice house. A little smaller than the Pentagon but worth a good deal more. I put it at about five million dollars worth of stucco and orange tile and flower baskets. Made you realise just how big the craze for video games was.

I followed Susie inside. Dark, cool, polished, smelling of lemons. Lots of huge Indian rugs, Indian art, pieces of art – paintings, pottery, sculpture – from south of the border down May-hee-ko way. Brahms gently wafting from concealed speakers. We kept walking. A maid in the kitchen looked up, went back to chopping on a board. We went out onto a flagstone patio no larger than Dodger Stadium and in the middle distance there were a couple of people artfully arranged in lounge furniture at the poolside.

One appeared to be the ultimate California girl: tall, broad-shouldered, slim-hipped, long streaked blonde hair. When she got up you knew what the songwriter meant when he inquired if you'd ever seen a dream walking. She stood up, full-breasted in a knock-your-eyes-out bikini as we approached. There was a guy with her. He had that roundly muscular physique I associated with Samoans whose names no one but football coaches could pronounce. Dark glasses, bathing suit like a slingshot, heavy towel around his neck. Earphones. He was listening to one of those tiny tape players and when he stood up the wire connecting him to the tape sort of pulled one of his

21

ears askew and the tape player fell off on the stones and he looked frightened, confused, and then embarrassed. I was delighted.

'Darling,' Miss California observed, arms out. She hugged Susie gingerly. 'I'm all sticky,' she said. I could smell the oil.

'Mother,' Susie said. She looked at the muscular wonder, then ignored him. She nodded at me. 'This is Professor Prize, Mother.' She introduced us and I felt a firm, if slippery handshake. *This* was a mother? Only in California. If I didn't get a hold of myself I might wind up spending the whole damn afternoon looking at the breasts of the Griffin women.

'I'm Shirley,' the woman said. 'Oh, my . . . I've heard so much about you, Professor. Sue does think the world of your class. But I'm afraid she's brought you out here to no avail – you are the detective, aren't you?'

While she talked she was leading us to the shade of a large round glass-topped table with an umbrella like a circus tent. We sat. The throwin' Samoan had finally pitched the goddamn headphones into the grass and was glaring at us defiantly. I wanted to tell him that he and his problems were of supreme irrelevance to me. Shirley beat me to it. She crooked a finger at him and he came a bit closer. 'Why don't you go pump some iron, Eric? I'll be in later.' He began to move away. 'Don't pout,' she said, her laughter like a butterfly in the late afternoon sunshine. Purple jacarandas were everywhere. The stains looked like a trail of blood on the flagstones. Eric's muscles rippled. His whole back seemed to have a life of its own as he walked away. His purpose in the Griffin scheme of things seemed cruelly obvious. Shirley turned back as if he didn't exist. Susie had never acknowledged him. *When the end comes I know, they'll say just a gigolo, and*

22

life goes on without me . . . It struck me that if he could still get it up for this Shirley character he ought to get a chestful of medals. Combat pay. Blood in the scuppers.

I said: 'You were about to tell me why I've come out here to no avail. I'm still listening, Mrs Griffin.'

'Well, dear Sue is overreacting to her father's behaviour, I'm afraid. No, Sue, let me have my say. I'm sure you've told Professor Prize all your theories . . .' She must have been a bit past forty but her muscle tone was scary. Flat belly, legs smooth as ice cream, eyes bright and clear, hair silky and soft, no cigarette hoarseness. Impressive. Credit where credit is due.

'I think she may have represented your viewpoint pretty accurately, too.' I said. 'I just wanted to see if you had anything to add to what you've already suggested to your daughter. He either is off on a toot or he has disappeared: those seem to be the options the two of you have come up with. Seems to me that several weeks adds up to a fairly long toot.'

'Of which, believe me,' she said, 'Silas is quite capable. He's a man of extremes. Work six weeks without coming up for air, celebrate for six more. Energy to burn. Angles to play.' She shrugged and the teardrop breasts wobbled sensually. Sue was staring off across the pool. Maybe a bottle with a message from her father would come bobbing into sight. The breeze pushed the palms around. Enormous poplars rose at the perimeters of the lawn like walls too high to vault, keeping people out. Or in.

'What I'm really saying,' Shirley said, tapping a long nail on the glass, 'is that Sue has been a wonderful daughter to Silas, loyal to a fault, devoted in every way. And – frankly – she's been just a wee bit blind to some of Silas's peccadilloes. Many other girls before her have felt the same way about their fathers . . .

23

I'm not telling tales here, Sue, just being frank and honest.'

'Oh, God, not frank and honest again.' Susie sighed and stood up. 'I can't stand such overpowering candour and openness. I'm going in. Wake me when it's over, Matt. We've still got to get a plan in place.' She didn't sound particularly angry. More like she was bored with her mother's repertoire. Shirley smiled.

'Sue, darling, would you have Esther bring out some iced tea for Professor Prize and me? And if you see Eric, would you – '

'Mother, iced tea is one thing. But I have got to draw the line somewhere. Eric is somewhere. I wouldn't even hand the creep a note.' She headed off across the lawn.

Shirley was still smiling. I said: 'I like your daughter. Good head on her shoulders.' I couldn't believe I'd said that: I sounded just like the old vicar sucking up free tea at the manor.

'You have in all innocence, I assume, put your finger on part of the problem.'

'Who? Me?' I smiled ingratiatingly. I doubt if any sane man could have thought a woman who looked like Shirley Griffin might conceivably find him attractive. Still, you could hope. I was beginning to blither in my mind so I stayed with the smile.

'Older men. Silas is one – and Sue cannot imagine his doing anything wrong. She blames me for the break-up of our marriage. Don't judge me by yon Eric, Professor. He is a nitwit but I'm experiencing a second childhood. I married Silas when I was nineteen and seem to have missed my first childhood. Eric is the equivalent of messing around with the highschool football hero. In fact, if his knee had held up, he'd have been a football star at UCLA. Now he harbours ambitions of being a . . . don't laugh – a stockbroker.

I'm trying to ease him into real estate. In any case, there were no Erics lousing up my marriage. There was only Silas and Silas was plenty. He wasn't much of a lover, really. And he was obsessive about his work. And, to give him his due, he surely could make money. If I may be frank and honest with you, a woman can put up with a great deal if the price is right. In Silas's case, well . . . look around you. And don't quote *Ozymandias* to me. I know all about that. *Look on my works, ye mighty, and despair.* Well, I'm not in this life to leave a monument. Whatever I can enjoy here and now, I'm for it. Eternity can take care of itself.'

Esther brought a pitcher of iced tea and Shirley poured and I leaned back, listening to the ice tinkle in the glasses. It was the best iced tea I'd ever tasted. Had to be the surroundings.

'Older men,' I said. 'You were saying?'

'Oh, yes. Silas is one and Sue adores him. Can do no wrong. Now don't think me mad, but in Sue's terms you are also an older man.' She squeezed lemon into her tea, swirled it around, added a packet of Sweet'n'Low, waited, then sipped, licked her lips. 'She's told me a great deal about your class, how you were a private eye in Los Angeles – really quite a romantic figure in her eyes. She likes you. Do you understand?'

'No.'

'Of course you do. But I'll spell it out just for the sake of your ego – '

'Of all the things in the world you have to worry about – I've only just met you but I can name a handful right now – I'd say that the condition of my ego is way down the list.'

'Good Lord! Touchy!' She was grinning in a sensually predatory way: as many teeth as Diana Ross

25

and all the Supremes, crammed into one wide, hungry mouth. I had the feeling that nothing I could say was going to light up her diamond vision. She was the sort of woman who gave you the feeling that she was rolling you around her tongue while she decided if she wanted to bite. 'My point is just this – her interest in having you undertake this search for her father might merely be a ploy to spend some time with you.' She took a deep breath and my heart skipped a beat or two. 'Don't say you haven't been warned. She may think she's her father's daughter. But she's her mother's, too. I know how her mind might work.'

I shook my head and laughed. 'I'll admit it's a wee bit unusual. Back in the days of very great yore when I was a private eye, there were more wandering daughter jobs than you could keep straight. I met a lot of very worried fathers. But never a wandering father job with a worried daughter. You seem wonderfully unconcerned, Mrs Griffin. Does that make you one very cool bitch or what? No offence, I'm just joining in the spirit of frankness – '

'I understand perfectly.' Her lustrous eyes twinkled. 'I am probably sort of a cool – no, make that cold – bitch when it comes to Silas. A charmless fellow. But if I thought he might be in any great difficulty, I'd want him to be helped out of it. I honestly believe he's off in the hammock with three or four Mexican whores and a case of the best tequila and some very expensive cigars. I hate to see my daughter, whom I love in my own fashion, waste too much of herself on him. He won't return her investment. I know him. He's a perfect louse, Professor.' She decided to bite, cracking the ice between those molars.

'What does your son think about all this?'

'Bart? Bart has nothing to do with any of it. For God's sake, leave Bart out of it.'

'All right. Do you particularly mind if I humour Susie to the extent of looking at Silas's boat?

'Oh, come on, Professor! You'll do what you want, so why ask me? If I were you, I'd want to stay as far away from the slightly messy life of the Griffin family as I could – and that would include poking around on Silas's yacht without his permission. He might just sue your ass off if he's in a bad mood. But it's his boat, not mine. Whatever you do, *bonne chance*. I have the feeling that you'll need it. People who wander into our lives often do – '

'Is that a warning, Shirley?'

'Damn straight, Matt.'

I had to laugh. Thing was, she meant it.

Chapter Three

I left Shirley Griffin languorously massaging tanning lotion into the firm flesh of her golden thighs. The sun was dipping past the poplars which made her efforts seem a little unavailing, to use her word, but when I looked back one last time she'd stretched out at a corner of the pool where the sun was still bright. She glowed. She lay as if composed for the grave.

In the kitchen I found Esther still chopping and asked her if she'd let Miss Griffin know it was time to go. She frowned at me, her heavy Mexican face collapsing in downward arcs, as if she had proof of my activities as a white slaver. I smiled and went back out the way I'd come. The house was so perfect you had the feeling that they all did their living somewhere else. I guess that was the point of maids and cooks and butlers and gardeners, creating the illusion that there was no one messing everything up. How the hell would I know?

I stood by my little red heap, noticing that the orange rust was clashing with the paint job, when something caught my eye. It was a hummingbird, a stationary flicker of colour, and then I refocused and through the window well past the hummingbird I saw a shadow which resolved itself into Eric. He was peering out at me, dark and rippling, and didn't seem to mind that I'd caught him at it. He kept staring, motionless, and I waved. Nothing. Maybe he was watching the hummingbird, too. Finally he moved away from the window and Susie was coming through the huge front doors, across the tiled verandah.

She'd changed tee-shirts. This one was navy blue and the lettering was in yellow:

> *There is a tide in the affairs of women*
> *Which, taken at the flood, leads –*
> *God knows where.*
>
> *– Lord Byron*

'That's my favourite so far,' I said.

'Dad gave it to me. He said Lord Byron sure had a fix on women.' She was still carrying her Yo-Yo Ma bag but had put on a pair of tight tan gabardine slacks. I kept trying to get a rear view without being obvious, since I would never do anything gauche or obvious. Unless absolutely necessary. This was one of those times. I walked around behind her and whistled loudly. What can I say?

Fortunately she chose to ignore me. 'Come on,' she said a trifle impatiently. 'If you think there's some point in checking out the *Baja Dream,* let's go do it.' She got into her own car and looked back at me. 'I suppose you lost your reason when you were alone with mother.' She started the Mercedes, looked at me expectantly.

I placed my palm on my forehead, waited. 'No, it's still there. Thank God.'

I followed her back down the hill, envying them the view they faced whenever they left Castle Griffin. The bay lay peacefully before me, a few boats bobbing, framed by the palms and the clouds and the curved arms of land speckled with white and tan dwellings among the greenery. Definitely an Impressionist scene. The only flaws were the black, spindly oil derricks poised on the water like birds of prey, just out of reach, taunting us. Lew Archer wouldn't have liked that either.

I watched the sun glinting on her blonde head in front of me and wondered if Mom had known what she was talking about. Could Susie really be pursuing the issue of the disappearing father just to spend some time with me? It was possible, I supposed, remembering all the little chats she'd arranged to have after class and in the snack bar, the eyes connecting in the Rathskeller. But . . . but – it didn't really make any sense. Kids weren't shy, anymore. If she had a fling on her mind it was more likely she'd just sit down and tell me about it and ask me what I was going to do about it. She hadn't made up the disappearance of Silas Griffin. The guy was gone. The question was just, was it his choice and innocent? Or somebody else's? Or an accident?

And besides, when it came to pretty girls figuring out ways to spend time with me – I didn't have that kind of luck. Hell, *nobody* had that kind of luck.

She took a sharp turn into the parking lot and damn near lost me. I wished she'd pop for the new signal light. The lot was asphalt, full of cars certain kinds of people are willing to sell their souls for, surrounded by chainlink fencing. We went through a gate where the keeper knew her, nodded, and then walked out a long pier with all those millions of dollars worth of pristine white hulls lolling in arms reach. With the sunshine on the water and the white paint and the funny rippling, underwater kind of shadows, you could go blind.

At the end of the pier a couple of guys were talking, leaning on the railing. They had the look of forced intimacy of strangers doing a drug deal, at least from a distance. Up close I had the feeling that the shared intimacy was of another kind altogether. One looked like the kind of college quarterback who gets the twenty million dollar deal the day he's drafted by last season's NFL doormat. Big, tan, light brown hair cut neatly, and a face – when he turns it on you – makes you think of guys in TV movies. Hunks. The expression on the face was cool, pretty, empty, and the eyes looked right past you like a man thinking about finding the open receiver in the end zone.

The other guy was wiry, short, very dark. He looked like the girl you wished your boy was taking to the prom. All except for the black moustache struggling to establish a foothold above the delicate, curved lips.

'Hi, Tod,' Susie said to the quarterback. He nodded and when she told him my name he gave me one of his soulless looks. He stuck out his hand and when I shook it I noticed that something was all wrong. His hand weighed about twenty pounds. The wristbands I'd thought were mere affectation were actually weights, strengthening his wrists for some doubtless awesome physical activity. He was wearing shorts and a tee-shirt which had no middle. I hate guys like that but you have to be careful with them. They can turn a regular guy into catfood real quick sometimes. Tod Yaeger also had doughnuts around his ankles, so each step he took strengthened his legs. If he kicked you you'd probably get familiar with the St Vincent's ER pretty soon.

'We're looking for Dad. Have you seen him lately?'

It turned out that Tod was not merely in training, killing time. He owned the marina. Aside from the ancient dead eyes, he looked awfully young to have pulled off such a big score, but it was California and lots of people seemed to find money in the bushes. Lots, if they were right kind of bushes. But he hadn't seen Silas Griffin in recent weeks. 'One day I just didn't notice him anymore. Couldn't tell you when he actually left. Things kinda creep up on you and you realise you haven't seen anybody for awhile.'

'That's life,' I said, nodding. The little cute guy with the moustache had moved a few feet away and was listening, staring down into the water at his reflection. 'Have you gotten any cheques for the space from him since he left?'

Tod looked at me pityingly. 'Mr Griffin doesn't pay *monthly*. None of these people pay *monthly*.' Having reduced me to a quivering jelly, he turned back to Susie. 'Wish I had seen him, Suse. What's going on?'

'I just need to find him.' Now she was playing the snotty rich bitch, dismissing the help. One for our side. 'I'm going aboard, Tod.'

'You bet, Suse. Takin' her out?'

'Of course not.'

She brushed past him and climbed on board and I followed, feeling Tod's eyes like icecubes on my back.

I've never owned a boat. I seldom find myself on a boat. I do not, by and large, trust boats. Look at the *Titanic*. They are – it is part of their karma, one might say – inevitably associated with water. I can't swim. I know nothing about boats. To me it's *front* and *back*, not *fore* and *aft*. *Wall*, not *bulkhead*.

But all I needed to know about this boat was that Silas Griffin wasn't on it. I made a quick tour of the deck, found no body of Silas Griffin and nary a drop of his blood. Susie opened the door – she called it a *hatch,* God bless her – and we went downstairs, into a cabin fitted out like a kind of rec room. There were several video screens with consoles, keyboards, joysticks; several pc's from a variety of manufacturers, stacks of notebooks. But it had all been straightened up as if by someone who was planning to go away. And if he meant to go away, the way I saw it, we didn't have a problem. Silas Griffin was a grown man and could go where he pleased, whatever his daughter might think.

Susie shrugged. 'I told you he wasn't here.'

'Just hold on a minute. What are all the other rooms – '

'Bedrooms, galley, nothing special. I looked in all of them a week ago – '

'Well, since I'm here I'll take a look, too.'

She sighed frustratedly. I followed her down the hallway. Companionway. Corridor. You get the point, right? The doors were unlocked. Everything was spick and span. No dirty dishes with telltale fried egg stains in the shape of Bolivia. No words scrawled in a runny yolk naming the murderer. No body. The place looked like it was for sale.

Until I asked what the last little door was. Susie said it was a kind of utility closet which contained a washer and dryer, spare parts for the boat, ropes, buckets, lights, probably a secret wireless to reach the Nazis or the rumrunners. I told her I really wanted to see that stuff and she did everything but stomp her foot, straining at the leash. I wasn't quite sure where she wanted to go next. But she opened the door, wheeled, and marched off down the hall so she'd be ready just in case I ever wanted to leave.

Which made her miss the main event.

She was absolutely right. There was a washer, a

33

dryer, all the spare parts and all the boat stuff. And a lumpy roll of canvas.

Thing was, two feet were sticking out of the roll of canvas. Nice shoes. Tiny feet.

I huffed and puffed unrolling the damn thing, curiosity overcoming my fear of stiffs. I know, they're dead, nothing to be afraid of. Call me crazy but dead guys scare me. This one wasn't as scary as some, I admit. He wasn't very big and one look told me he wasn't Silas Griffin.

This guy was at one time your distinguished Mexican. Back in those good old days he was about five feet six, lots of wavy hair with matinee idol grey at the temples, swarthy, rather coarse-featured, but a bit of a looker. But that was all a week or so ago. It had been a rough week. He'd aged a lot. It had been hot as hell in the utility closet, for one thing. A good shower with Dial wasn't going to make him smell good. And he was a dead loss as a talker.

He was wearing a blue blazer with a crest on the pocket. I recognized the insignia of the San Amaro Country Club. Pale beige linen slacks, those cute little shoes, a pale lavender polo shirt, and a fish scaling knife jammed into his chest. As an ensemble it worked fine until you got to the knife and all the clotted blood and the disconcerting smell.

I heard Susie scream and I damn near fainted.

She'd come back to see what was taking so long. She had looked over my shoulder, saw the mystery guest, and grabbed me while making a loud noise.

'My God! It's Freddie Sanchez!' She flung herself back across the narrow hallway as if she'd received an electric shock. Her face had the blank, white look of sudden shock. She had her forearm up across her mouth, just like the girls on the covers of the old pulp magazines. Same kind of chest, too, now that I think of it.

'Freddie Sanchez!' I cried, thinking I should know the name. But I didn't. 'Who's Freddie Sanchez? Why is he cluttering up your father's utility closet?'

She was blinking at me, her mouth moving. No words were coming out. I shut the door and pushed her down the hall and up the stairs toward the fresh air on deck. I always feel so hopeless when women faint. Or men. I told her to take a deep breath. I wanted to offer her the Reese's chocolate cup that was gooing up my pocket but something told me it wasn't appropriate. Tod Yaeger and his friend had moved back down the pier toward the big marina-centre. Yaeger looked back, saw us, and looked quickly away.

'So, who is Freddie Sanchez?' I said. She was leaning against the railing, swallowing hard.

'I'm not exactly sure,' she said haltingly. 'He's a Mexican businessman. I met him at the country club this summer. Dad's the membership secretary and I play golf and tennis there. I partnered Freddie in doubles a couple times. He was so bouncy, so quick on his feet, making little jokes under his breath . . .' For the second time that afternoon she was struggling not to cry. I figured she'd had about enough for one day.

'Was he a friend of your father's?'

'I never heard one mention the other. They weren't the same type, you know? Freddie was sort of into the arts. Dad wasn't into much but computers.' She fumbled a tissue out of her Yo-Yo Ma bag and dabbed at her eyes, blew her nose. I kept thinking of Shirley saying that Susie liked older men. Silas, me. And now Freddie. Silas had vanished. Freddie no longer had a speaking part. I didn't much like the implications.

'Silly of me to ask, but you didn't happen to see

35

the corpse when you were checking the boat a week ago?'

'What a question!' She giggled nervously, not wanting to cry again. 'No. But I didn't actually look in the closet – '

'Right, right. Well, I don't know how long he's been dead. But there's no question now – we're going to have to call the cops.'

She nodded numbly. 'What about Dad?'

'We'll get to that, but murder takes priority.'

We walked back toward the marina to make the call. The gulls were screeching overhead. It was feeding time.

They probably smelled Freddie.

Chapter Four

Phil Redding was the only cop I'd ever met in LA who hadn't looked at me like he wanted to shoot me. Obviously he was out of step with his colleagues. He wound up in San Amaro which gave him more time for his boat, which was small, and his golf, which was pretty good and not played on the pricey fairways of the Country Club. He was the senior man on the San Amaro force of which he held a fairly low opinion. He was fond of saying: 'May any force but the San Amaro force be with you.' Officially he was the Chief, reporting to Mayor Gonzer. He was in his early to mid-forties. God had intended him to be bald. I can't imagine how ridiculous he'd have looked with hair. His dome was freckled and tan and there was hair above his ears and running around the base of his skull. He reminded me of Robert Duvall if Duvall were sort of Clint Eastwood tall.

When I got the call through to him he was happy as a kid with a new Gremlin doll to commit mayhem with. You didn't get many murders in San Amaro, particularly murders which were mysteries. Usually it was the wife or the husband. You had no doubt that Freddie's wife had stabbed him and left him to die in Silas Griffin's laundry room.

Susie and I waited at the *Baja Dream* until Phil arrived with an elderly traffic specialist by the name of Jenkins. I went down to have another peek at Freddie and watch Phil do his stuff. It didn't take him long. He said his scene-of-the-crime guy was on his way with the box of goodies. He also said that spending much time with Freddie in his present condition could put you off your feed.

We went back on deck where Jenkins was telling Susie that murder was interesting but if you wanted real excitement you had to try and control the traffic during the weekend of the San Amaro Festival. Redding went through all the standard questions with Susie and me, taking it all in: Susie's concern about her father's disappearance, my involvement, her mother's lack of concern in light of her former husband's normal behaviour, Susie's previous meetings with the late Freddie Sanchez at the Country Club. I could see the way his mind was working. This might not be just a murder. Silas Griffin's boat was involved, therefore so was Silas Griffin. And Silas Griffin had a certain star quality in some circles. And he might be the subject of a missing persons hunt at any moment. His frown at the smell downstairs was turning into a grin of anticipation.

We chatted a bit about the turns of fate that had brought us to San Amaro and he said we didn't have to hang around when I told him that Susie had had a fairly difficult day. Go on home and I'll get back to you. He was as far from the standard dick-hating cop you could imagine. He could get mean but never just out of habit. We left. I thought I'd better make sure Susie got home okay.

The sun had set, the lights of San Amaro were draped like a necklace on the throat of the bay. The smells of the sea and all the vegetation seemed to blossom at night, flooding you with saltiness and sweetness, thick, almost like a gentle drug. It was cool

38

and clear as we drove up the hill, through the clutching palm tree gate and past the geyser of water in Silas's lake. The windows of the house glowed dimly yellow, comforting, and I could hear Stan Getz samba music drifting softly from speakers on the verandah. There were people who actually lived this way. My reaction was as simple as I could make it. I wanted to be one of them. Pact with the devil, selling off a few government secrets, anything. But the Devil had never made me an offer and I didn't have any secrets. Shit.

Shirley Griffin was sitting alone in the perfect living room. It was almost dark. A couple of tablelamps burned on distant tables. A couple of logs flickered in the huge fireplace. A gesture to the September evening. She was drinking champagne. The bottle sat in a hammered silver bucket which was sweating. Stan Getz's saxophone was as beautiful as she was. There was no sign of Eric. He was probably snoring somewhere, an empty discard.

We told her what we'd found. She was a good listener and made us drink champagne with her. 'I don't mean to make this look like a celebration,' she said. 'Poor dead man. But I suppose we're celebrating the fact that it wasn't Silas – '

'We still don't know where he is,' Susie said. I could tell from the sound of her voice that she hadn't shaken the sight of the body. She'd really lost her fizz. Like someone had unscrewed her top and left her on the counter. I wondered why: was it just the murder? How well had she known Sanchez, really? 'We've still got to find him.' She gave me a tired, pleading look and I nodded.

'Now that Redding's involved I'll talk it over with him – '

'But I want *us* to do something,' she said.

I ignored the look Shirley Griffin shot at me. 'We will, we will. But the last thing I want to do is get in Redding's way. Just be patient another day, Susie.' I turned to Shirley. 'Did you know Sanchez?'

She shook her head. 'Never heard of him.' She sipped champagne and crossed her legs. She was wearing a shapeless white cotton dress. It looked absolutely drop-dead, as they say. It couldn't be easy being her daughter, no matter how pretty you were. 'It all seems rather painfully obvious to me,' she said. 'Your Mr Sanchez was on board for some reason of his own, he probably had an appointment with Silas. It was late at night, the marina was deserted, a couple of drug runners decided to steal a boat for themselves . . . and found Mr Sanchez, instead. Bang, you're dead.'

'He was stabbed, Mother.'

'Stabbed, then. Random violence. Isn't that the most plausible explanation, Professor?'

'Beats hell out of me,' I said.

I left not long afterwards.

I was awakened the next morning by yet another blonde. This one was breathing hard, covered with sweat. Just the way I like 'em, I thought with a tigerish grin. She was leaning over me. I could feel her breath on my face. She kissed me and I tasted the sweat on her upper lip. My eyes were shut. I was helpless, a mere plaything for this wanton creature. Then she began beating on my head with a newspaper.

I didn't have to open my eyes. It was Jan. She was wearing her dark blue running shorts and a Los Angeles Rams sweatshirt. She was sopping wet from running five or six miles on the beach. She was back so it was about seven-thirty. Jan. I was much too good for her but I'm a chap of easy virtue, an easy lay. She used me shamelessly and I was powerless to stop her.

God, nothing but a tissue of lies. Try again. She was an heiress. I was poor. We spent many happy hours together sharing our hobbies, earning merit badges together. We slept together. I'd have married her in a flash but she clearly had too much sense. I kept telling her I wanted to get my hands on all that money while I could still enjoy it. She wrongly believed that I was unprincipled. I tried to make her see that my principles were as good as the next man's. If the next man were an unabashed gold digger. My first principle: money was to be spent. We tended to go 'round and 'round on this subject. She had just opened a bookstore in San Amaro. Lots of mysteries. The fact that I'd been a private eye had – for a day or two when we first met – made me seem glamorous in her innocent eyes. I'd soon put an end to that.

'You're in the paper again,' she called from the bathroom. She turned on the shower and, like all women, kept talking and could never understand why I couldn't hear her. I think they do that on purpose, so they can tell themselves how stupid men are. The one who'd attacked the Land Rover with the VW had *always* done that and would *never* repeat what she'd said. She should have been institutionalized.

I opened my eyes, struggled into a sitting position, and looked at the paper. Some twerp had taken a picture of Susie, Redding, and me on the deck of the *Baja Dream*. I hadn't even noticed the flash. But there we were. And the story on the front page got the facts more or less right. Nothing about looking for Silas Griffin. Just references to his ownership of the yacht. No explanation as to why his daughter and I were on the yacht. Just the fact that we found one dead Sanchez whose address was given as Mexico City.

41

There was a paragraph about my involvement in a case a while back, shortly after my arrival in San Amaro, and the statement that while I had once been a private detective in LA I was now teaching criminology at Cal State. No libel, no slander, so there went my grounds for a major lawsuit.

Jan came out of the bathroom wet and naked and I got up to pee. When I came back she was still damp and naked. She was in bed, crooking a finger at me. Grinning like a mischievous little girl. She was twenty-six. Maybe she was the Devil. Maybe this was the big offer. I asked her and she said sorry, no, it wasn't. Being so congenitally easy, I got back into bed anyway.

Later I sat at the kitchen table watching her pour hot water from the kettle into the top of the Chemex coffee maker. The fog from the beach came in through the windows and the salty smell blended with the freshly brewed coffee which was a mixture of Kenya and Vienna roast. It finally got the smell of Sanchez out of my head.

She was wearing panties. She looked at me and said: 'So what's with your running around on yachts with pretty co-eds?'

'Co-eds,' I mused. 'Don't much hear that anymore. It's like *moron*, another of my favourite words.'

She just stared at me.

'It's a long story – '

She said: 'Funny. I have plenty of time.'

So I told her and we drank coffee and I ate a bagel with some cream cheese and lox that had been in the fridge a day too long. She never seemed to eat unless we went out to dinner or made an occasion of it. A dyed in the 100% pure wool health food nut too.

She also made a sweep of the cottage every so often, throwing away my hordes of chocolate. Not a woman to fool with.

'So you didn't find her father. You did find a corpse. Typical.'

'I also found Mrs Griffin. Or whatever she calls herself.'

'How could I forget? The young Lauren Bacall, I believe you called her.'

I nodded. 'Yes, I believe those were my words.'

'You know that the untold riches I represent to you grow ever more distant. I mean, you do know that? And sometimes I think you're actually getting close . . .' She shook her head sadly.

'Sure, you say that now. Cheap blackmail, I call it.'

'Call it whatever you will.'

'After what just transpired in our tiny bed? You can talk to me in this tone? Jan, you should be ashamed of yourself.'

'Quite possibly I am. When will you unmask the killer?'

'When will you marry me?'

'Men your age are so hot to get married.' She shook her head, sipped her virtuously black coffee. 'Did Silas Griffin kill him?'

'I don't know. I'll ask him when I find him.'

'You are going to keep looking?'

'Baby, I have to. How else could I keep an eye on the Griffin women?'

Would she actually have poured the coffee into my lap? I like to give her the benefit of the doubt. But we'll never know. The telephone rang.

It was Phil Redding.

He told me that they'd spent the night doing a search of the yacht and checking on the corpse. Freddie Sanchez turned out to be Frederico Sanchez,

43

a highly respected art expert and a curator of an important museum in Mexico City. He asked me if any of that rang any bells with me and I said no.

'Look, you busy?'

'Don't be coy, Phil. What's up?'

'We found something else while searching the yacht. You want to come down and take a look?'

You can't turn down that kind of invitation at the start of a murder investigation. I figured the more I knew about what happened on that boat, the more I might know about Silas Griffin. And that was supposed to be the point of the exercise for me.

I told him I'd be there in an hour.

For half an hour Jan and I went back to bed and contemplated the meaning of life.

Chapter Five

From outside the San Amaro police HQ looked a little like a fancy motel beckoning to the weary traveller. It was stucco and stone, low and flat-roofed with a little gable over the entry, elegant splashes of bougain-villea among the carefully landscaped shrubbery. An American flag snapped in the morning breeze as the sun began to burn at the fog. Halfway down the block stood City Hall, a more traditional example of official architecture, where Mayor Gonzer was kept chained to his desk. It is said that raw meat is hurled in Gonzer's direction a couple times a day but I dispute that. Surely no more than one feeding a day. Being hungry is what keeps him his charming self.

When I saw Redding at his desk I had my illusions wiped rudely away. His office was the same bilious blue-green of most police stations, though I had to admit this one didn't have the smear of blood which had decorated his LA hutch. His desk was scarred with cigarette burns and chips where louts had banged their hand-cuffed wrists. He looked like a man who had been up all night and then breakfasted with Gonzer. He saw me, coughed for a while, shook a Camel loose from its crumpled moorings, stuck it in his mouth, and flipped his Bic. The smoke seemed to calm the cough.

'Shit,' he said thoughtfully. 'Headache. This

morning I'd pay extra for the Tylenol with the poison in it.' He blinked at the smoke. His eyeballs were stitched with crimson. The bags beneath the stitches were purple.

'Lookin' good,' I said cheerfully.

'I've been up the whole night and then Hizzoner wanted me to report to him at breakfast.'

'Uncanny,' I said softly.

He didn't hear me. He went on balefully. 'Mrs Griffin called me last night. Late. Said she'd been thinking. Told me she was sure this Sanchez was a drug runner . . . he was trying to steal the boat and had a falling out with his cronies and they killed him. Why not?, I thought to myself. Then half an hour later I got the word on Sanchez.'

'So? He could still have been running coke up the coast – '

'I dunno. I don't think so. I think he's for real. *Was* for real.' He yawned and peered into his coffee cup. It said PHIL on the side. Just in case he forgot who he was. He flipped ash into the cup. 'An art guy. I ask myself, why does a Mexican art guy get iced on a computer genius's boat? In my town? Why?'

I couldn't think of an answer. 'So you mentioned you found something,' I prompted him. 'Smells awful in here. Why don't you ever open a window? You should be glad you got a window – '

'What? And stink up the whole damn town?'

When Phil gets despondent there's no dealing with him.

'What did you find?'

'You know a lot about art, right? You're a professor – '

'Oh, come on, Phil. What am I here for?'

'Art,' he said. He stood up and stretched. 'Did you

46

ever watch Gonzer eat fried eggs? Makes my blood run cold. Come on, take a look at this stuff.'

He led me down the hallway toward a room with wire mesh instead of a front wall. He unlocked the door and we went in. I looked back out at the hallway. This was how a monkey at the monkey house felt. Enough to drive you to bananas.

He was opening a large box. He took out three objects in large baggies and placed them on the table. 'Go ahead, take a look. We've gone over them for prints. Too damn many prints to make any sense. G'head.'

Three small paintings in ornate gold-leaf frames. Lots of gold in the paintings, dark blues, deep burnt umber, all very stylized. They looked old. I studied them for a few minutes while Phil had another coughing fit.

'Whattaya make of them, Professor?'

'Listen, I'm no art expert, but . . .'

'Amaze me. But what . . .'

'These are icons. Dates back to the Eastern Orthodox doctrine of veneration. Icons were central to the religious experience of the time. On the one hand, we see them now as pure art but that's not what they started out being. At one time they were the Classic Comics of their day. They instructed the uneducated faithful in the stories of the Bible. New Testament. In the Byzantine and Orthodox tradition the icons were symbolic – I'm putting this badly but they had a practical function. They expressed visually the theology, the teachings, of the church. These two show the Virgin and Child guarded by some kind of sentries. Maybe the sentries are supposed to be saints or something, I sure as hell don't know. This other one seems to be Christ with some more saints. I'd say they're pretty typical, very formal, face on depictions.'

I shrugged. 'Not bad for a private dick, right? I must have taken a class once.' I smiled proudly, surprised that I knew anything about them at all.

Redding arched his back and grimaced. 'I'm impressed,' he sighed grudgingly. 'Doesn't take much to impress me, remember. When it comes to art I'm more into the calendar from Harry's Tyre and Auto. These things worth much?'

I shrugged. 'How the hell should I know? I suppose it depends on how old they are. If they're the real thing I suppose they're worth plenty. I think there's a pretty sizable market in newly painted, antiqued icons but they're sold as souvenirs, not as the real thing. They're not forgeries. They're copies. What these are, I haven't a clue. You'll have to ask an expert.'

'Next on my agenda.'

'Where did you find these?'

'On a shelf in the utility room. Right behind a box of fabric softener. Thing is, they were wrapped in the same kind of canvas as the body of Mr Sanchez. Sailcloth. But the *Baja Dream* doesn't use sails.'

'Don't look for a sailor, my friend. Look for a painter. This sort of canvas is more likely to be used for oil paintings. So you've got the beginnings of a nice little case, Phil. You've got three icons which may or may not be the real McCoy. You've got a dead museum curator. And both the icons and the corpse were wrapped in painter's canvas. Tell Gonzer you'll be making an arrest before noon.'

'Not funny.' He opened the door to the cage and waited for me to go back into the hallway. He locked the door behind us and walked back out to the waiting room and booking area, then into the lobby which was largely for show. The guy at the desk was fresh and clean, a PR man's dream. He went outside with me and stood blinking in the daylight. 'We'll check with the museum in Mexico City. Might be some of these doodads – '

'Icons,' I said.

'Icons. Are missing. Maybe Mr Sanchez was in business for himself.'

'Maybe he was,' I said dubiously. 'But whoever killed him must have gone away empty-handed.'

He raised his eyebrows. 'Who says? Maybe we just found the last three doodads. There mighta been dozens.'

He was right. I hadn't thought of that.

Chapter Six

The art angle was all very interesting but I wondered if maybe two cases were developing. If so I'd have to be careful to keep my own case in the forefront of my mind. We had Sanchez and the icons in one column: there was always the lure of a murder. The adrenalin got pumping and you wanted to keep digging until you uncovered the truth. It was fun. But I wasn't looking for a killer. I was looking for Silas Griffin who'd been gone for weeks and who wasn't supposed to number iconography among his enthusiasms. They were linked only by the murder scene – Griffin's yacht, the *Baja Dream*. And Griffin hadn't been on his boat in a long time. Two columns. And only one connection. Too many times I'd seen dicks diverted from one case to another and then you didn't know which way was up. Nothing made sense. It was like old Jake Gittes used to say. When nothing made sense, it was Chinatown. You couldn't figure it out.

When you're a private cop you live and die by your connections. That was why Phil Redding was important to me in the old days. You had to know a cop or three, cops who trusted you. And you dared never betray a confidence. The next best thing to a cop on your side was a newspaperman. They live in a world of their own, just like cops, and once you had a friendly one he was worth his weight in gold. Norm

Levine was a friendly. We'd met when he was in LA at the *Times*. He'd left to rusticate in San Amaro but stayed in touch, played chess by mail just for the hell of it though we were still only an hour's drive apart. We were both baseball fans. He was a Cubs fan and I was willing to suck down a martini or two with him and listen to him reminisce about Bill Nicholson and Peanuts Lowery and Phil Cavaretta and Andy Pafko and Hank Sauer. He'd been a kid reporter and because somebody was out sick he'd gotten to cover the Waitkus story – when the fancy fielding first-sacker took one in the belly from a mysterious lady. Right there in the Windy City. From then on Eddie Waitkus was his favourite ballplayer and when he recovered and came back to win the Comeback Player of the Year award no one was more excited than Norm. We still drank to Eddie on the anniversary of the gunplay. Norm was that kind of guy. Tradition meant a lot to him.

Living in LA was never quite as exciting as Chicago for Norm and God only knew where San Amaro ranked on his scale of excitement. But he'd mellowed into middle age by becoming just a bit of a hippie. Frizzed his hair, got a divorce, took a pottery course. And smoked a joint or two when the mood was upon him. He was to the San Amaro *News-Hour* what Phil Redding was to the San Amaro cops. He made it run. What he didn't know about the town and its citizenry you wouldn't want to bother with. Consequently, when I'd gotten it clear in my mind that Silas Griffin was my main concern, I knew I'd have to buy Norm lunch.

He got free about one o'clock and I was sitting on the deck at Ratso's, a joint cantilevered out over the beach down a blacktop road from the Pacific Coast Highway outside of town, when he came putting along

51

on his motor scooter. He was wearing his crash helmet and when he took it off his hair exploded like a dandelion puffball. He wore his usual jeans, Nikes, and corduroy jacket. He'd grown a long wispy moustache that made him look like one of the James gang.

He slid into the chair opposite me, looked at me through the flat black lenses of his aviators, and said, 'Amigo,' to me, and, 'Anchor Steam,' to the waitress. He spoke very softly, like a man who knew so many secrets he had to be constantly on his guard that he might be overheard. He grinned up at the sun and said: 'So, you're in the shit again, amigo. Always believe what I read in the paper. But why were you on the boat in the first place? You and the Griffin girl an item?'

'Such a suspicious mind.'

'No, just dirty. Professor out on the family yacht with the daughter, a student no less. Dead guy. A whiff of scandal. Dirty. Logical. But we here at headquarters keep an open mind. What's your story? You thought she could get you a discount on a video game?'

The waitress brought his Anchor Steam beer and a Margarita for me, a bowl of nacho chips and hot stuff. The breeze was cool and the sun was hot and the fog was gone. Gulls flapped and yelled and sunbathers and surfers were showing up.

'Old man Griffin has gone AWOL and his daughter's worried. She's taking my criminology course, knew I'd once been a dick, and turned to me for help. Don't laugh like that. It's beneath you. Silas has been living on the *Baja Dream* since his divorce a year ago so we went there to find him. Or a clue to where he might be. Came up empty on clues but found a body. But I keep telling myself not to confuse the issue –

52

I'm just helping the girl look for her Daddy. The murder's something else again – '

Norm laughed and shook his head. The hair made him look like a man from another age altogether. He pulled on the beer. 'Don't kid a kidder. The girl and the Daddy come with the murder. The chances of there being no connection . . . infinitesimal. So don't spend much time bullshitting yourself. You want to have me give you a rundown on the Griffin clan, I assume.'

'In exchange for a lavish lunch.'

He didn't bother to look at the menu. 'In that case, I'll have the abalone.'

I told the waitress to bring two abalones and damn the expense.

He began by telling me some of the general outline of what I already knew. Then he got to something I didn't know.

'Then,' he said, slowly enjoying the abalone, 'there's the whole business with Bart. The son. I looked up the file this morning before you called. Refreshed my memory. This was before you came to our fair city where there is no crime and the livin' is easy. Son Bart is what's known as the lull in the conversation.'

'I mentioned him to Mrs Griffin yesterday and she practically had a fit. Told me that Bart had nothing to do with any of this and she wanted him left out of it – '

He nodded, chewing. 'Excellent abalone, by the way. And a perky little vintage.' He sipped at the California chablis which had taken the place of the beer. He patted his mouth and mustache, leaned back, and took a cigar from a leather case. He offered me one, a great brute of a thing, and we lit up, the smoke drifting away in the breeze. There was a dog barking

53

to someone on the beach to quit messing around and throw the goddamn stick. 'Bart ran into a spot of trouble a while back, got himself thrown in the pokey. It's one of those convoluted stories and you just can't pin down the truth. The way Bart told it, he was innocent as an egg fresh laid. Old Bart and this chum of his were out having a few belts one night when a fella came up to them, bought 'em a drink, struck up a conversation. Older fella, real friendly like. Turns out he needed somebody to jockey his boat south to the Baja while he drove down. Said he'd meet 'em there. Simple job for a couple of guys who knew their way around boats. And for their trouble and time he'd pay 'em five bills apiece. At least this was Bart's story after the roof fell in. The Coast Guard saw it all a little differently.

'The Coasties stopped the boat off San Diego and boarded it with what they called "cause." They found what they called "traces" of marijuana in the storage lockers and both of these fine upstanding lads were arrested – '

'Whoa!' I said. 'The boat was going the wrong way! Who the hell ships marijuana south?'

'The Coast Guard claimed the boat did a fast one-eighty when they caught sight of the intercept party. They further claimed that they saw the two men dumping the marijuana over the side. It was a stormy night and they never found the dope and the Griffins hired a top gun lawyer from San Francisco to do his number. The case went to trial but the boys were acquitted. Their story was just as good as the Coast Guard's. Better, really, because Bart's mother testified that he'd been at home the previous night and couldn't possibly have gotten to Mexico and back in the few hours he was gone. She apparently convinced any doubters and Bart and his pal walked. This was three, four years ago when Bart was twenty-one, just the age his sister Sue is now. But while the jury believed Bart that didn't make him aces with his father. Apparently Silas and Bart had a big falling-out and Bart left home. Silas kicked his ass right out of there.'

I nodded. 'I got the impression that Bart wasn't around much. Where is he now?'

Norm shrugged. He was picking his teeth with the edge of a matchbook. 'Ya got me. He hasn't been in the news since then, the file's empty.'

'The guy who hired them to take the boat south, did he ever turn up?'

'The boat was registered to a man named Aaron Withers. Malibu type but he was represented at the trial by his lawyers who said that Mr Withers was in Europe and that the boat had been stolen. Withers remains, at least officially, an innocent bystander. A footnote to the case.'

I tucked into a wedge of chocolate pie and coffee. 'Well, it sounds to me as if Bart and his pal were probably telling the truth. They were innocent bystanders, too. Even if there was contraband on the boat. Just one of those things, bad luck.' Maybe I just didn't want to drag the Griffins any deeper into the mess.

Norm sighted at me down the length of the cigar. 'You are just not as suspicious as you were once, my boy. But I thought the boys just got caught in somebody else's scam. Now I'm not so sure . . .'

'So? So? Come on – '

'Well, last year the other young man was back in the news. Right here in San Amaro.'

'And who is he, pray tell?'

'Kid named Tod Yaeger. Bought the whole damned marine. Makes you think, doesn't it? Fella twenty-four, twenty-five, where does he get that kind of money?'

He just gave me that sly newspaperman's smile. He was right. It made me wonder.

Chapter Seven

Eugene Francois Vidocq.

He's the guy who began this whole thing. He was born about 1775 and was one hotshot villain. He did a lot of things. Pitchman, sailor, soldier, puppeteer, convict, cop-hater, master escape artist. He beat up a cop who seduced his girlfriend and went to prison for it. He kept escaping. Once he got away in a policeman's uniform. Another time he made a death-defying leap from a prison guard tower into a swiftly running river. In the end they put him in chains and hard labour, and he spent several years getting to know his fellow convicts, among whom were various representatives of the Cornu family who educated their children in the way of murder and used to let them play with the heads of victims to get them used to the idea of corpses.

Finally he escaped a third time and the Paris police never caught him again.

Instead, about 1810, he'd tired of making a living as a used clothing dealer. His old pals kept threatening to betray him to the officials if he didn't do right by them. They had the goods on him, no doubt of that, so Vidocq took himself off to the very heart of the matter. He went to the cops himself and made a deal. He would turn over all his information about the

Parisian underworld if they'd scratch the accumulated prison sentence hanging over him.

From such a humble and even notorious beginning came the Sûreté, the oldest criminal investigation institution of its kind in the world. Vidocq set up headquarters in the Petite Rue Saint-Anne and staffed his force with former convicts. In 1812, while Napoleon was having his own troubles which later inspired the late Mr Tchaikovsky to compose his celebrated *Overture*, Vidocq and his twelve ex-cons arrested 812 murderers, burglars, embezzlers and whatnot, but also cleaned up dense packs of criminals where no French inspector would ever dared have ventured before.

By 1833 Vidocq's anonymity was shot and he resigned. He was a legend by that time. He promptly founded a private detective agency, the first in the world. In his spare time he was an entrepreneur, writer, and friend of Balzac. Balzac acknowledged that Vidocq supplied him with frequent ideas for stories. He died in 1857, eighty-odd years old.

So, he started it all. Vidocq, the first private eye.

Time passed and along came yours truly. Onward and upward, *excelsior*!

I mention all this merely because I had a lecture to give when I left Norm Levine and it didn't require much preparation on my part. Vidocq was my hero. The kids ate it up.

All except one.

Susie Griffin wasn't taking any notes. She had a distracted look on her pretty, perky face, and I knew she couldn't wait until I'd finished with Vidocq. Which I finally did, giving them a teaser about Alphonse Bertillon who was only twenty-six in 1879 when he joined the Préfecture of Police of Paris and completely revolutionized the playing of the cops-and-robbers game.

They all filed out of the room and left Susie staring at me. She was wearing a lavender tee-shirt which I read:

> *You can pretend to be serious;*
> *You can't pretend to be witty.*
> — *Sacha Guitry*

Probably a gift from a TA in Higher Metaphysics. I didn't ask.

She was concentrating on being serious, not witty. There was just the hint of a lower-lip pout as she stood staring at me.

'Are you still working for me?'

I laughed. 'I still intend to do a favour for a friend, if that's what you mean. Come on, let's get out of here and I'll answer your question.'

We went outside into the sunshine and sat on the grass beneath a tree. I was wearing my seersucker suit and my black-and-white saddle shoes and a pair of bright red Brookstone fireman's suspenders she couldn't see. Just as well. I felt very collegiate and was optimistic to match. It wasn't Phil Redding. It wasn't even Norm Levine. It was Eugene Francois Vidocq. He always made me feel better.

'So what's going on? Mother said she talked to that Redding guy last night. I'd gone to bed. Mother's phoning her ideas in from Mars, as usual. I told her Sanchez was no druggie – I mean, did he look like one to you?'

'No. He looked more like an museum curator from Mexico City – '

'But how – ' She stopped abruptly and made a funny little face, swallowed, and looked away. 'How would you ever come to a conclusion like that? Do curators have particular characteristics? Did you notice gold leaf under his nails from handling priceless frames? Bits of paint scrapings?'

'Would that it were so. But that Redding guy told me the fact of the matter this morning. He was up all night diddling with the Mexico City police based on the ID he found and got a make on the guy. Which said he was an art curator.'

'What kind of art? Not that it matters, I guess – it can't have anything to do with Father – '

'Maybe it does, maybe it doesn't. They found something else on the *Baja Dream*.' I told her about the icons and she nodded and I asked her again if she could make any connections between her father and either Sanchez or the artworks. She wasn't giving anything away but she'd shown something when I'd hit her with the identity of Sanchez. I could have pressed her on it. But I didn't want to scare her off. I could always come back to Sanchez, who wasn't going anywhere. More important was the feeling I was getting that maybe she wasn't quite so innocent as she'd at first appeared. By the time they're her age women are almost never as innocent as they might appear. Maybe I should have that put on a tee-shirt for myself. As Lord Byron used to say, 'There is a tide in the affairs of women which, when taken at the flood, leads . . . God knows where.'

'What are you going to do about my Father?'

'I'm going to keep asking questions. I'll keep you informed. But, Susie, don't start telling me how to do my job, okay? A few weeks of Criminology One doesn't entitle you.'

She looked sheepish and nodded. So innocent. Such

a little girl. Now that I'd gotten to know her I didn't notice the nipples poking at the tee-shirt. She wasn't just a good looking female anymore. She was a person. Just maybe she was a liar. That remained to be seen.

I told her I had some errands to do and she walked me back to the wreck. It baked in the sun, top down, and the seats were going to be hot. When I parked under a tree in the shade either the seats got sap or birdshit on them. The car had bad karma. Stephen King could have written a book about it.

'Look,' I said, throwing my jacket into the back seat, and catching her eye, 'you and your mother don't have much to say about Bart – '

'That's right. He has nothing to do with this. We're a little tense on the subject of Bart. How did you even know his name?' She frowned at me. 'Are you prying into our lives?'

'Don't turn into a jerk, Susie. Or I'll flunk you. His name came up during the course of my inquiries about your father – you're going to have to face up to the fact that you're all caught in the same web. The web of the family. No getting out of it. I know about Bart's misadventure with the Coast Guard and the blow-up with your father so don't waste time pretending it didn't happen. See, this is the part about getting involved with private heat that can make you wish you hadn't. I'm just wondering where old Bart might be hanging out these days – '

'You think he did something to father!' She looked truly startled and decidedly unhappy.

'No, no, no. Did I say that? I would just like to talk with him. You and he have the same father who may be missing. It's logical, if you think of it. And trust me.' I felt like shaking my finger in her face. 'Do you know where he is?'

'I wish I knew! He's such an irresponsible fool. Just

won't grow up and behave like a man. Keeps floating along on the current. I suppose he's up the coast somewhere, or down the coast – ' She shook her head impatiently. 'Probably living in a van with a bunch of hippies who don't know they're twenty years too late.' Listening to her made me think of Lew Archer confronting the rootless kids on the California coast in *The Zebra-Striped Hearse*. One of his best cases when you thought about it. Essence of Archer.

'You sound worried,' I said. 'Are you afraid he's involved?'

'Involved in *what*?' she flared at me. 'Make yourself clear. Involved in my father's disappearance or the murder?'

'You tell me,' I said calmly. 'You're the one who looks worried.'

'Oh, damn it! You'd be worried too if he were your brother! He's that kind of person – always skulking around the edges of something weird. He's never going to grow up, that's all! And we – mother and I – we're both worried about him. And the problem between Bart and my father, *our* father, went a little further than just a bawling out. You know?'

'No. I just heard your father threw him out after the acquittal on the drug running charge. What happened?'

'They came to blows,' she said almost primly, as if she were repeating a line of dialogue from an old movie.

'Explain.'

'Bart took a swing at Dad. That was a mistake. My father was a boxer in college. He moved right in on Bart and hit him twice in the stomach. Bart fell down and threw up. Dad gave him a towel, told him to clean it up, and get the hell out. It was a pretty bad scene. Bart said a lot of things before he left . . .'

'You could have told me that Bart and Tod Yaeger were chums. It'd be nice to know these things – '

'Don't be silly. We weren't dealing with Bart and Tod – why would I bring that up?'

'Well, it's past now. Did he and Tod stay friends after the trial? Did your dad know Yaeger?'

'I don't know about Bart and Tod. Dad knew Tod at the marina, I suppose. But we didn't exactly spend a lot of time reminiscing about all the good old days with Tod, if that's what you want to know.'

I wasn't going to argue with her about everything. And I was getting tired of conducting what amounted to a cross-examination of a hostile witness.

'How do you think Yaeger got the money to buy the marina? Family money?'

'I don't think he has any family money,' she said.

'Maybe it was drug money,' I said.

'I don't know,' she shrugged, looking very small and vulnerable. 'Mainly what I know about Tod Yaeger is that it drove mother crazy having Bart hang around with him. Absolutely crazy!' She batted her big blue eyes at me, as if to say, Who can explain the behaviour of mothers? She looked at her watch. 'Oh, God – I'm late for class. When will I hear from you?'

'Soon,' I said, as I wondered if the Snicker bar in my glove compartment was melted beyond edibility.

Chapter Eight

It had been twenty-four hours since I'd first seen Shirley Griffin but, truth to tell, she didn't look a day older. The sun had been swallowed up by some purple late afternoon clouds rolling in off the ocean like billowing smoke. The lights were on in the house and Esther was polishing more copper bottomed bowls and pans than you could find in your favourite three-star frog joint. I didn't see any signs of Eric. Maybe it was his day off. Maybe he was studying for his real estate exams. Maybe he'd gone back to Samoa.

Shirley Griffin was wearing very preppie Bermuda shorts and a little white blouse and muddy white gloves. She was holding a trowel like she knew what to do with it. She was weeding a flower bed. Without looking up, she said: 'There's gin, tonic, lime slices, and ice on the table. Make two, will you? Heavy on the gin. It's been that kind of day.' I did as I was told and she said over her shoulder: 'How are you, by the way?'

'In need of a drink, now you mention it.' I clinked ice and poured and swirled and brought one of the drinks back to her. She lifted it in her muddy glove.

'Absent friends,' she said and grinned wearily. She really was a beauty. How did that kind of woman get such an even, silky tan? Or is that a mystery that is merely meant to exist, not be answered? 'Catch the killer?'

I shook my head. 'Shot down a couple innocent civilians, though.'

'Don't kid me. There are no innocent civilians.' She leaned back, sitting on her heels with her thighs spread. She was sweating in a dainty, ladylike way. She blew out a deep breath. 'I've had it. The curse of a green thumb. You keep doing over again what you pay the gardeners to do. Do you garden, Professor?'

'I don't think so. Unless you count growing some marijuana – you know, in a small, non-commercial way – in my extreme youth gardening. I don't think I do.'

'I call it foolish. If not actually criminal. But then I'm something of a hardliner on the subject of drugs.'

'Better pour out that drink, then,' I said.

'Oh, God, don't be irritating. Please.'

'I won't if you won't.'

'Okay, okay. I confess. Give me a hand, help me up.'

I gave her a hand and I liked her touch. Jan would hate this woman. She'd have good reason. I kept remembering that Shirley Griffin was not only divorced but rich. One of your better combinations. Plus looking like a blonde-streaked Cyd Charisse. Be still my heart. She tugged on me and levered herself up. She wiped at a drop of perspiration on her nose and left an adorable little smear of mud. I wanted to kiss it off. Soon I'd be writing couplets. It figured. She probably had bumped off both Sanchez and Silas. I felt a raindrop, big and soft and warm.

'I take it you came here to talk to me,' she said. She gave me a level, appraising look and much to my surprise I was still capable of audible speech.

65

'No. I thought maybe Eric would like to arm wrestle.'

'How amusing.' She walked over to the table and sat down in the shelter of the huge awning. The rain was beginning to fall. 'You're going to get wet.' I went over and sat down across from her. The rain was pattering on the awning. For some reason being out in it but protected by the awning made me feel like a kid. 'Funny you should bring Eric up. A feeble witticism but coincidentally it was Eric that made my day a bit of a trial.'

'Well, you know what Sacha Guitry said.'

'I'm afraid you have me there.'

'You can pretend to be serious. You can't pretend to be witty.'

'I suggest you take his advice to heart, Professor.'

'So what happened with Muscles?'

'You might say I put up the closing notices. The show had no legs. He disputed my decision and I had to insist. The conversation grew heated. I told him to turn in his keys to the 450. I had Esther call him a cab. He left in low spirits. At the top of his lungs.' She sighed, examining her nails, finding a chip. 'Life is so hard.'

'Except for the very rich,' I said.

'You have a point. I won't argue with you.'

'If you ever sell this place, maybe you could list it with him. Just a thought.'

'Frankly, I don't think Eric has a future in real estate. However, he is gone, a fading and somewhat embarrassing memory, and you are here. What is it you want with me?'

I thought of several things which I tactfully kept to myself. The rain made the place smell like fresh earth and sexy flowers. 'I'd like to speak to your son,' I said. 'Try to cut the bullshit and just tell me where he is.'

'Who do you think you are, talking to me like that?' She didn't raise her voice or make an angry face. She asked the question softly, as if she simply wanted to know if I thought maybe I was Napoleon or Christ or Mr. District Attorney.

'I'm someone your daughter has turned to for a favour. I didn't come looking for aggravation.'

'We didn't invite you into our lives. We didn't ask you to pick and poke and pry – ' There was some fire in the eyes, that was all. She swirled the ice, sipped, took a long drink, and poured some more gin on top of the tonic. The rain was spattering my face. It felt good.

'Susie invited me into your lives – '

'I told you. She probably wants to sleep with you.'

'That hoss won't run – '

'Don't be so sure. It wouldn't be her first fling with an older man – '

'Oh, please. I'm not that much older. I may be younger than you – '

'Gallant, too,' she said, raising her eyebrows. 'And I am her mother – which would make you an older man. This is becoming an idiotic conversation.'

'I just asked you about Bart – '

'I do not intend to discuss my son and our family affairs with you. I don't even *know* you.'

'No, and if you keep hounding me this way I doubt if you ever will.' I smiled my village idiot smile.

She laughed. 'It's hard to imagine your amounting to much as a private detective.'

'I gave them a feeling of over-confidence.'

'That I can believe, Professor.'

'So why didn't you like Bart hanging around with Tod Yaeger?'

'Who told you that?'

'It's common knowledge. Waitress at the Coastal Coffee Shop told me – '

She had decided to ignore me when I pretended to be witty. 'I suppose you got poor little Sue talking. She trusts you.'

'What did you have against Yaeger?'

'Surely it's obvious if you've met Mr Yaeger.'

'Be a sport. Spell it out for me.'

'He's a homosexual. Gay.' She said the word as if she'd bitten down on a lemon.

'Well, I'll be darned,' I said.

'Bart was very impressionable in those days. He thought Tod a rather glamorous figure, trendy, stylish. Into all the new music. The new clothes. I didn't want anything weird to happen to Bart and Silas – well, if Bart had come home with an earring – Tod affected an earring at one point, I believe – I think Silas would have ripped his ear clean off. Silas's values tend toward the traditional. God knows, the business with that boat and the Coast Guard was bad enough. I mean, *bad* enough . . . so Bart has been something of a prodigal son.' She looked at me again, all sincerity. 'Now, does that satisfy your curiosity?'

'My curiosity is incurable,' I said.

'Terminal, in other words.'

'Do you think the boys were running dope?'

'Obviously not. They were innocents drawn into something they couldn't control. If there were drugs on that boat, they couldn't have known and couldn't have put them there – '

'What about the boat's owner? What was his name?'

She shook her head, shrugged.

'Withers,' I said, 'that's it. Aaron Withers. Ring a bell?'

'I guess that was his name. Do you think he might have been the one who hired the boys?'

'I understand that he denied it, said the boat was stolen. How would I know?'

'You were willing to jump to conclusions about Sanchez. He turned out to be Mr Respectable. Museum curator – '

She shook her head dismissively.

'You always suspected that Bart was guilty, didn't you?'

'I'll tell you what I always suspected, Professor. I always suspected that Tod Yaeger was a slimy creep. I think that maybe Tod knew what they were getting into and he wanted somebody along for the ride . . . but I don't think Bart knew a bloody thing about what was going on.'

'And why was that?'

'Ask Yaeger.'

'Maybe I will at that,' I said.

We sat in silence, listening to the rain. Then she stood up. 'I think the interview is over. You can sit here until the gin and tonic are all gone and the ice bucket is empty and you're soaked to the skin. I'm going to take a hot bath. Goodbye, Professor. And . . . be careful.'

I sat at the table for a little longer, finished my second drink, tried to see the pieces of the puzzle clearly, but somehow I couldn't do it.

I needed more pieces. Finally I got up and went looking for some.

Chapter Nine

There's an air of futility about a marina in the rain, huddling beneath the blackening clouds. The yachts sat deserted and useless like so many statues, bobbing, the water sucking noisily at the hulls. The marina shops were pretty well battened down and the neon signs cast a ghostly pink glow in the falling rain. What had such a spiffy, sharp look in the bright sunshine looked vaguely tacky and dripping. The only activity centered around a pizza and hotdog counter where a couple of teenagers with bikes were talking to the highschool girl pulling the Coke handle. I wandered over carrying an unhappy umbrella I'd found under the front seat of the VW. One of its ribs had cracked and gone west and the fabric was pulled all to hell. So far as I knew, it was the only umbrella I owned and it was a surprise.

I asked for a pepperoni slice and a Coke and asked the girl if she'd noticed if Tod Yaeger was around. She didn't know but one of the boys said there was a light on in the office and he'd seen Yaeger tying up some loose ropes in case the wind came up. He acted like he knew what he was talking about so I nodded. My slice came from a warmer oven and the tomato sauce tasted like a hotdog. I asked the kid where the office was.

He pointed around the corner and his pal began to

giggle. 'You better call before you go to see him,' he said and they both guffawed, very much men of the world out on the town. They were maybe fourteen.

'And why is that?' I asked.

'Because he's got *company*.' They looked at each other, trying to keep straight faces. 'Y'know, like one of his friends.' I wasn't giggling with them. 'You know Yaeger, mister?'

'Met him. That's it.'

'Well, he's got his pal Quin with him. And – '

The girl behind the counter interrupted. She gave them stern looks. 'All they mean is, Mr Yaeger may be in a meeting with Mr Jefferson. You really should call.' She looked down at the half-eaten slice on the paper plate. 'It's awful isn't it? Makes you think they must *try* to make it that bad. Would you like a chili dog on the house?' She smiled and brushed stringy hair out of her eyes. There was a smudge of pizza sauce on her white blouse. She couldn't fool me, though. Put her in a bikini and get her out on a sunny beach and she'd be a California girl. Magic.

'I'll take a rain check,' I said, 'but thanks.'

'There's a pay phone over there.' She pointed.

'Oh, I don't want to interrupt Mr Yaeger. I can always stop by tomorrow.' I pushed off from the counter.

'I'll remember a freebie for you, okay? You won't even have to ask.'

'You'll never recognize me without the umbrella,' I said.

She laughed and as I walked away I heard them all buzzing and she was giving them hell about talking about Yaeger that way.

I made as if to go toward the parking lot but stopped when I was out of their view, made a sharp right, and headed back around the other end of the building

71

toward the office. It was always better to drop in unannounced, particularly on guys who had little vulnerabilities. The office had a cute little shingled stoop, as if some misguided architect had wanted to introduce a little bit of old New England to the project. The lights in the office shone behind the blinds which were closed. I just opened the door and walked in.

If I'd been hoping to catch Yaeger and Quin Jefferson in anything approaching a compromising position I was disappointed. Yaeger was sitting behind a big desk sorting through a stack of correspondence and the other guy was leaning back in a chair with his cowboy boots on the edge of the desk. He was reading a paperback copy of *The Winds of War*. From the condition of the book I'd say he'd been at it for quite some time. My money was on Wouk to outlast him, wear him down, and win on points. Quin Jefferson looked like Tyrone Power in *The Black Rose*. Very shiny black hair, sculpted brows, a sensual but open, trustworthy face. Much of the time I look like a dumptruck just parked on me. I cannot stand guys that are prettier than Shirley Griffin – a newly formulated law.

Yaeger looked up, surprised. 'What the hell – '

'How are you, Tod,' I said, smiling, shaking off my pathetic umbrella. Quin Jefferson eyed me slowly over the top of his book.

'Oh, hi . . .' He was thinking. 'You're . . . ah, the guy with Suze, right?'

'You got it.' I looked around the office which reminded me of a dying, off-road motel. Who cared what the marina's office looked like? It was a rental and management office, what did I expect? Interesting as this dialogue with myself was I turned back to Tod. 'Everything seems pretty calm around here, considering there was a murder. All that stuff in the papers.'

'Well, the guy wasn't one of *us*, y'know? And all the rain makes for a pretty empty place – we got one party going down in the Dogherty's slip, that's it.' He leaned back and took a bite from a granola bar. 'So what can I do for you?'

'Bart Griffin. I'd like to talk about Bart Griffin.'

He just stared back at me, expressionless. After a while he said: 'So . . . talk about him.' Quin Jefferson chuckled quietly, turned a page. He shifted the pale blue lizard skin boots. He wore a lot of gold. Bracelet, ring, couple of chain necklaces. He didn't look as though his body had ever given refuge to an ounce of fat, yet he wasn't skinny. Solid, lots of muscle tone. Not obvious like Tod.

'Well, I was just wondering if you saw much of him anymore. Thought you might have stayed in touch – you sort of owe him one, the way I figure it.' I leaned back against the door and watched my umbrella make a puddle on the carpet.

'I don't owe Bart Griffin anything. What the hell are you talking about? What have you got to do with Bart Griffin or Suze or anybody else? You come down here and I get nothing but trouble and sad songs. A murder. The cops. The newspapers. And now you're back – well, buddy, I don't have to talk to you – '

'Look, I see the barbells in the corner. I know how tough you are. It concerns me, okay? But it also concerns me and a few other people that you lured Bart into a pretty shady deal – hell, you were guilty as hell that night, you ought to be doing time right now – '

He stood up. He was wearing a flowered Hawaiian shirt and pleated chinos and he looked like he used a fairly vivid blusher. His nose was straight and pointy and I wondered how it would feel as it flattened out. I smiled at him, nodded to Quin Jefferson: 'You keep questionable company, young fella.'

Yaeger told me that I was full of shit. 'And that whole business with Bart is over and done with. We were found innocent and you've got no business coming in here and raking it all up again. Now get the hell out!'

Jefferson was looking very serious now. He'd folded down the corner of his page and put the book on the desk. He'd tilted forward in the chair and had his feet on the floor.

'Who were you working for that night, Tod? You might as well tell me . . . I may be able to keep it under my hat. But like I said, there's a lot of renewed interest.' It was all nonsense, of course, but Tod was just another guy with a guilty conscience. Accuse most people of having done something bad and they'll remember what it might have been. No kidding. 'New evidence could get that sucker opened wide up again. Next time they might just drop you through the floor for a few years. Fella like you, you might be real popular in prison . . .' I grinned, ashamed of myself. Where did I come up with lines like that? Probably from sitting in on enough police interrogations in LA. 'Who were you working for that night? Was Aaron Withers the man who hired you? Guy who came up to you in the bar and asked you to run that boat south? Was that the story? Or did you run it down the coast, make a pickup and start back before the Coast Guard spotted you? Was Withers the guy financing the drug trail?'

I was so far out in leftfield I couldn't see the pitcher. My accusations made no sense but Yaeger couldn't be sure. And, then, maybe Bart hadn't been home when Shirley said he had. Maybe she was lying and if she was then I might be closer to the truth than I had any right to be. Mainly I was just enjoying pressuring this guy. I was indulging myself. I kept thinking: how could this character afford to buy the marina? So I asked him, boring in.

'Drug money, Tod? That's dangerous. For you. But I don't give a shit about you, come to think of it. Somebody turns you into fishfood, so what? Right?' I smiled good-humouredly. 'Just tell me where I can get hold of Bart . . .'

'Go to hell,' Tod said, glancing at Jefferson, who was still watching me. He had tiny ears and I noticed the glimmer of a gold earring in the top of one. His sideburns were cut geometrically, like daggers. The more I looked at him the more he was looking like a spiffed-up punk, not Ty Power at all. 'Now get the hell out of here. For all I know you killed that spic on Griffin's boat – '

'Beautiful,' I said. 'You're a beauty, Tod. Think about what I've told you – you could save yourself a lot of grief by helping me find Bart and his father – '

'Out!' he screamed. 'I don't know anything about any of them. Now, out!' Ropes were standing out in his throat and he was restraining himself with some difficulty. He'd probably read that I'd been a private eye and was afraid I might have a gun. Or maybe he just wasn't the violent type. Quin Jefferson watched the two of us with total lack of involvement. When I left he was already picking up his book again.

I didn't go back to the car.

I got to thinking about the party on the Dogherty's boat. Maybe someone at the party might have known Silas Griffin, might have been a pal. People at a party were usually willing to talk. So I set off down the pier. It was still raining and the wind had picked up, kicking spray underneath the remains of my umbrella.

But this wouldn't take long. Any leads on Silas or Bart would be worth getting wet for. Since I'm the sort of lout who hates any inconvenience I could only figure that I'd gotten hooked by the case. Hooked by Susie and Shirley was more like it.

All the yachts were dark and wet and closed up but for one where the Dogherty's were entertaining a few friends. They were wearing foul weather gear and sitting outside. They had a roof over their heads but they were getting wet from the sides and seemed to be pretty excited about it all. They were grilling steaks and drinking wine and making salad and I hated to intrude. But I did. They knew Silas and Shirley, all right, but only in passing and hadn't seen much of them since the divorce. Not much help.

But as I was leaving their company, having had a beer and some Double Gloucester on rye bread, Ned Dogherty followed after me.

'Look,' he said, 'I didn't want to get on this with the girls listening. Get it? This sorta thing makes them a little jumpy. But the thing is, Silas had a girl . . .' He looked at me, wondering if I was up for a confirmation.

'Quite a few, from what I've heard,' I said. 'Like his romance with booze. Went on binges with the ladies, too.'

He was shaking his head. 'No, besides that. I think he was getting pretty serious about one certain girl. I saw her on the boat a few times, always just the two of them. Grilling steaks or fish, sitting talking . . . Silas always needed somebody to talk to, somebody to run his ideas by, and this girl seemed to like that role. He introduced me once, one Saturday morning, they had their arms full of groceries and were laughing

76

and stopped to say hello and . . . hell, I forget her name. Rhoda? Rita . . . Something like that.'

'She didn't happen to mention where she was from, did she? They might have gone to her place . . .'

'No, we didn't have a conversation. Just hello. She was very pretty. That's about all I know.'

I thanked him and he went back to the party. One step closer, I figured. A woman. One Silas was taking seriously. Chances were he hadn't gone off whoring, after all. Four to one he was with the woman, telling her all about his dreams and plans and what the future held.

I was heading back along the pier. The pizza counter had closed up and the lights on the high standards gave the whole place a lonely look. The noise of the Dogherty party carried only a few feet and I was alone.

Then a shadow moved out from behind a stack of rigging and boxes of provisions.

'Yaeger told you to go away. But instead you go bother our clients. Why is that?'

'Well, Quin, this may come as a hell of a shock to you, but only one of us takes orders from Tod Yaeger. It's not me. So I guess I'll talk to anybody I feel like talking to. So why don't you run back to the boss and tell him thanks, but no thanks? Be a good little errand boy.'

I started to walk on but he jumped with disconcerting alacrity into my path. Oh, not this, I thought. I hate this. On the other hand I was also in sort of a bad mood and I was wet and fed up with my goddamn useless umbrella.

He grabbed my arm. 'Why don't I take you back to the office and you lay all that on Tod yourself?'

'Come on, kid,' I said. 'Let's not do this – '

He smirked.

I swung the umbrella across and hit him in the face with the exposed rib, saw it rake across his cheek. He grabbed his face. I used the umbrella like a bayonet and drove the point into his belly. Not too hard, mind you. He made a noise somewhere between a sob and a belch. Bent forward. But the umbrella was gone. I hooked my left foot behind his right cowboy boot and pushed his shoulder. He fell down and I should have figured I was a TKO winner and gotten the hell out of there. But I hadn't mixed it up with anybody in a long time and it felt good. Particularly since I hadn't hit him. Hitting people, particularly in the head, plays absolute hell with your hands, movies to the contrary. So I stood gloating, trying to think of a tough guy witticism. But as the man said, you can pretend you're serious, you can't pretend you're witty. I took too long.

The little bastard was off the deck in a flash with a knife from his boot. He came at me fast, practiced, and the knife rammed through my seersucker coat, my oxford cloth shirt, and my flesh too damn close to a rib. I felt a nick, a slithering sting and the warm flood of stickiness. The time had come to cut the clowning around. I grabbed his arm, twisted it hard, pushed him face forward against a piling. I slammed his face into the piling a couple times. He turned around and I held the point of the umbrella right against his groin. 'Think twice,' I gasped, 'because I am well and truly irritated.'

His face was all bloody from his nose. He judged just how hard I might be able to ram him, just how good my aim might be, and was this all worth it. I jabbed at him. He looked down. I jabbed again. He was mine at this point. He'd lost whatever edge he'd had with the knife. I pushed him backward with the umbrella and he slipped and fell into the water. He was clawing at the slick hull of a boat. He was choking. He was swearing.

'Next time I see you,' he bellowed, spitting water, trying to grab hold of a piling, 'you're dead, man, you're dead. I cut your heart out, man. Remember! Dead, man . . .'

I looked down at him. I said, 'Punk.'

The whole scene did my heart good.

I was sitting at the kitchen table at my place and Jan had put a frozen pizza in the oven as a big concession to me. It just wasn't my night.

She was also dabbing alcohol on my wound which was a painful process. I debated trying to impress her with my stolid manliness. Then I began whimpering. Man's gotta do what a man's gotta do.

I told her what had happened and she reacted with the proper outrage. She also thought I was an idiot to have been such a jerk in dealing with Yaeger and Jefferson. I told her that the code of the detective made it all right for me to push guys around, if only to stay awake. She snorted and jabbed some more alcohol into the wound and told me she liked me better when I was whimpering and vulnerable.

We drank beer and ate the pizza, which was a travesty, and then I went to the bedroom closet and felt around on the top shelf for the damn thing. I finally found it, all wrapped up in an old piece of sheet, and brought it back to the kitchen table.

'Oh, not that!' Jan slammed her beer down on the table and it slopped onto the pizza. 'You're not serious . . .'

It was a snub-nosed .38 snuggled down in its holster. I'd used it in the old days. I'd even shot a guy. He lived but that was all right. He'd been on my side. Mainly I'd used the gun as a prop to scare people. The guy who shot me, of course, hadn't been all that scared.

'Look, it's just for protection,' I said.

'Just carrying it makes you three times as likely to get shot yourself – '

'You just made that up.'

'Who cares? I don't want you carrying that thing – '

'Look, a nasty little creep with a knife told me a short time ago that he intends to cut out my heart the next time we meet. Well, hell . . . next time I might not be carrying my trusty umbrella. I can't punch my way out of a paperbag. I'd better have my gun. You know, just to fire a warning shot . . . come on, Jan, you don't want me to be nothing but a target. Gotta have Old Reliable under my arm.'

She fussed and I promised that under no circumstances would I shoot one of the good guys again. As a matter of fact, I've never been willing to accept the blame in that incident. Was down in San Pedro, lots of guns going off, cops and Feds and the villains and there was a nasty rumour that I had blasted a Fed just to prove a point. Nonsense, says I. And they never found the slug so it was never more than a rumour. An accusation. It was true that I'd never liked Slattery but then, who had? I might have shot him. But not on purpose. No way. Not me. They used to call him Slats. Now they call him Gimp.

'Do you think this Quin person killed Sanchez?'

'I don't know. Why? A curator? But he is handy with sharp objects . . .'

She bandaged me up with gauze and tape and dragged me off to bed. She started kidding me about Old Reliable. She promised she'd be gentle.

80

Chapter Ten

The next morning – yes, I had to buy him more food, in this case a very involved pecan roll and three cups of coffee along about ten-thirty – I went to Norm Levine for help. I'd been kicking the whole business around in my mind while I slept and upon regaining consciousness I knew I had to deal with the fact that, like so much of life, what started out simple was rapidly getting complex. I wanted to help Susie find her father and before I knew it I was waltzing around a rainy pier with a guy trying to stab me. The thing is, once you take the first few steps away from simplicity it's next to impossible to stop – you're not *anywhere* at that point – and even harder to crawl back to the safety of ignorance. So, you pushed ahead, determined that with only this one more step you'd clear the whole thing up and scuttle back to real life. The joke, dear reader, is always on me. I'm not getting closer to the solution, my goal. I just keep getting further and further from simplicity and happiness. And when the answers come, they usually leave you flat on your back with tyre marks on your shirt.

However. Still thinking I could take just that one more step and get everything sorted out, I bought Norm his week's ration of carbohydrates and suggested that it might be nice if we had a look for the goods on one Aaron Withers. Norm snorted, dunked a huge boulder of pecan roll in his coffee, and said he supposed he'd have to save my skin again. 'How much you getting paid for this job?' he inquired.

I shrugged. 'Friendship, that's all. I'm above mere money.'

Norm shook his head sadly. 'Loser, baby. Such a loser.' The sun shining through his hair gave him the appearance of an angel complete with halo. He was smoking a cheroot which accentuated his Jesse James thing. We walked back to the *News-Hour* and began looking through the morgue.

Norm always figured that there might be a story somewhere and if all he had to do was let me look in some old clip files, well, why not? Aaron Withers had two files. One because of his involvement in the Griffin/Yaeger matter with the boat, the other because the paper kept a Malibu section on prominent citizens.

There wasn't much in the file relating to the use of his boat by the young men. Withers's story was that he was out of the country and knew nothing about it until he got word that the Coast Guard had impounded his boat and wanted the answers to some questions. Everyone seemed to believe his story. He didn't look like a probable when it came to running coke and whatnot up the coast. Dead end, there.

But . . . aha! The way these things come together! A little bit here, another little bit there. It keeps you going, keeps you from heading back to simplicity. With each piece, the whole thing grows more and more tantalizing.

Would you believe my surprise to discover that Aaron Withers was on the board of directors of the LA County Museum of Art? Further items informed me that he had at one time been a major jade collector and had finally consigned his entire collection to the Walker Art Centre in Minneapolis, famed for its important jade collection. But he had other interests in the world of art. He collected early twentieth century sculpture, owned pieces by Picasso, Henry Moore, Giacometti, Brancusi, and apparently defined the early part of the century by whatever he wanted to buy.

And finally. And finally he was known for his fine collection of Byzantine art, especially . . . icons. What else? Being a detective is fun when things go right. Less fun when you look back on punks armed with knives and you with only an umbrella – though even that was fun while it was happening.

Norm looked at me and grinned slowly. 'You're not good, amigo, but sometimes you're lucky.' He blew out an immense amount of smoke and brushed his hands through his vast frizzy hair, about a bushel basket's worth. 'First you have little blondie, that's one. Then you have Silas, two. Mommie appears, three, putting her own personal hunk through his paces – Eric or whatever his name is, that makes four. Bart's name comes up, five. You find a stiff, Sanchez, six. Tod Yaeger is tied to Bart and the marina, seven. He's got the cutie with the knife, Quin What's-his-name, eight. And Aaron Withers who ties into the drugboat number and the art thing with Sanchez.' He was ticking things off on his fingers. 'Only one problem, amigo. None of it makes any sense. As my aged grannie used to say, it don't signify.' He was laughing and shaking his head when I left.

Hell, why was I going to all this trouble?

I drove down the coast highway toward Malibu with a low grey sky hovering just overhead, the kind of cloud cover the gulls would just disappear into and then come diving hell-for-leather out of, scaring the unwary beachcombers half to death. It was the sort of grey that makes you feel old and damp and sort of weary. The kind of day you begin to understand why people just said the hell with it sometimes, left their clothes in a little pile on the beach, and tried to walk to Hawaii.

The mood wasn't doing me any good so I pulled off at a roadside place where the ferns were swinging in the open windows and the coffee was hot. A couple of bikers were having beers in the bar and some seedy types were having coffee and pie, just like they used to back in Iowa. I wasn't hungry but had a bacon, lettuce, and tomato sandwich to show myself to be alive and taking nourishment.

Maybe it was the gun that was depressing me.

I hadn't worn it in a while and it was heavier than I remembered – both literally and figuratively, I'm afraid, heavy with memories I'd tried to put behind me when I stopped being a private cop. It was rubbing against the inside of my arm and I hadn't gotten it in just the right place. Maybe that would keep me from getting in the habit of wearing it.

Jan had given me hell about wearing it, too. Loused up breakfast. I didn't really blame her. In fact, I shared her attitude. But the simple fact was that I was afraid. What if that little creep came after me with another knife? The gun might scare him. It also bothered me that I hadn't put on the gun just to scare people. I made sure I put the bullets in. Jan watched me tight-lipped and silent. I told her if it looked like I might be getting into anything where I'd have to use the damn thing, I'd bail out immediately. She looked remarkably unappeased.

I went back outside and climbed into the rambling wreck. I promised myself that I'd check out Withers and if it didn't begin to get me some time with Bart or Silas I'd throw in my hand. That made me feel a little better.

I called from the Colony shopping centre and Withers wasn't in his office. Apparently he was an attorney with some other sidelights. Sounded like one of those rich, entrepreneurial types. His secretary said I might be able to reach him at home. His number was unlisted which was okay by me. I hate being turned down over the phone. I stopped at a drugstore, engaged a guy in conversation – young guy, looked like he was working part-time. I gave him some nonsense about trying to negotiate for Withers's yacht but losing his address and now what was I to do. Figured a local kid might know where he lived. He did. Thank God it wasn't actually in the Colony. The security guards have heard every bullshit story going.

Withers lived in one of those large places backed right up to the highway. You couldn't tell anything about the place. There was about six feet of width between the back wall and the whizzing traffic and I left the VW there, knowing that even if it got hit I might not notice.

His housekeeper let me in. She might have been Esther's sister though perhaps not as great a chopper. I told her to inform the great man that I wanted to speak to him about a mutual friend, Bart Griffin, and a subject of mutual interest, Byzantine icons. She listened impassively, looking like the weight of the Aztec past was weighing her down for the moment, and went away. I was standing in a narrow hallway, higher than it was wide. Three floors above, a skylight let the bright greyness pour through.

I heard her coming back. She seemed to be coming from very far away.

'This way, please,' she said. If O. J. Simpson had run behind her all those years Jim Brown's yardage record would be long forgotten.

She led me through a variety of rooms and hallways, the mood of the place constantly changing. One room looked like a law library, another like an elaborate ship's cabin with porthole windows, another like a formal French dining room with gilt chairs and gilt everything else. I got a look at several icons as we went and when we finally entered what promised to be the final stop since the ocean was rolling just beyond the open sliding doors, I got a look at the Henry Moore outside on the terrace above the beach. Hole in the middle. Couldn't miss it.

Couldn't quite miss Aaron Withers, either. He may not have been quite as large as the Moore but I'd have laid you six to five he outweighed it. There's always a fat guy, right? Usually a rich fat guy. Wears a white suit à la Sydney Greenstreet, right? Well, my rich fat guy was having image problems. He was wearing a pastel green dress. Okay. A caftan. But it looked like a dress to me. He was smoking the biggest cigar I'd ever seen. He was bald. Ageless, like a monument. Put a hole in the middle and he really would have been a Henry Moore. I suppose maybe he was sixty. Could have been eighty. Like I said, ageless, impervious to change. He was standing behind his desk holding a handful of darts. I stood there like a fool while he painstakingly threw them, carefully and with considerable accuracy, at a dartboard on a wall maybe fifteen feet away. One bullseye and the rest clustered around like pedestrians picking up change.

He turned, worked the cigar into the corner of his big pink mouth, and said: 'Who the hell are you? What kinda scam is this? Forget it if you got blackmail on your mind. I make a habit of admitting all my vices – there's nothing I'd pay to keep secret. Well, speak up, speak up!' His voice was a little high, a little on the piping side for someone so big.

'Frederico Sanchez,' I said.

He peered over his glasses at me. 'Funny. You don't look like a Sanchez – '

'I'm not Sanchez,' I said.

'Well, *I'm* not Sanchez. Perhaps this is all a case of mistaken identity. Whattaya think?'

'Wait. Let me start again. You're Aaron Withers – '

'I already know that.'

'I'm no one you know.' I told him my name, adding that I was an academic at San Amaro.

'You call that academia? You must be joking. What in the world do you want with me? I'm busy. Darts, my collections, my diet . . .'

'Did you know a Frederico Sanchez?'

'Not that I can recall.'

'He's been murdered. Up in San Amaro – '

'Don't look at me. I haven't murdered anyone in months. Look, my fine friend, you tell me you want to talk about Bart Griffin and Byzantine icons. Peculiar combination. But I figure, what's on this geek's mind – you being the geek. You got about ninety seconds before I start throwing more darts. Better get to your story.' He smiled. His teeth weren't so hot. Stained with nicotine, with spaces between them. A guy with so much money ought to have his teeth fixed. I'd been thinking about the house. Two and a half million, I figured.

'Bart Griffin. I need to know where he is.'

'A young man is found running drugs on my boat, stolen, and years later you come to my home to ask me where he is? This surpasses understanding. Am I to keep track of all the young hooligans on the west coast? I hardly recall his name – you amaze me, my man.' He regarded the ash on his cigar as if it were a pet he'd been nurturing. Then he tapped it into a cut glass ashtray.

'So, where is he?'

He kept a straight face. 'Works in a marine supply store in Santa Monica. On Wilshire. Pacific Marine and Scuba. Next question?'

I laughed. 'Very good, excellent! How come you knew?'

'I know almost everything, Professor. Even things that are not part of my life. When I wind up sending my attorneys at two hundred dollars an hour to testify in a case involving my stolen yacht, you may assume that I keep tabs on the people who got me into such a ridiculous position. You never know when you may run across such people again.'

'Then you also know about Tod Yaeger – '

'I know where he is, yes.'

'You know he bought that marina?'

He nodded his great dome of a head.

'You know where he got the money?'

He shrugged. 'Money is very easy to come by. I grow bored, Professor. You mentioned icons?'

'Thought you might know Sanchez. Somebody stuck a fishscaler in his chest on Bart Griffin's father's boat. Couple days ago – anyway, I found him a couple days ago. Turns out he was a curator of a big museum in Mexico City. The ensuing search of the boat turned up three Byzantine icons. Small. Maybe the real thing, maybe not. I kept adding things together – Bart, a boat, icons, you.'

'Hardly so sinister as you make it sound. Let me suggest that you have the icons looked at by a reputable expert. They might be of considerable value. They might not. One wonders why they were found in proximity to the late Mr Sanchez. But,' he stifled a yawn, 'one must also get back to one's darts. I wouldn't say you've wasted my time but you've come perilously close, Professor.' He stood up and padded out from behind his desk. He was barefoot and left a trail of dry sand on the carpet.

'Does this mean we're done talking?'

''Fraid so. God knows it's been a treat but all good things must come to an end.' He kept right on going all the way to the door. He opened it. 'Shortest farewells are best. Adieu.'

I had to laugh. 'Remind me to ask you for the name of your tailor some time.'

'Ah, you reveal the depth of your silliness, Professor. The wise man would want the name of my chef.'

When I left, relieved to find the VW in one piece – not an attractive piece, mind you – I was smiling and humming a happy tune. Aaron Withers was a rogue. Not many rogues left in our ordinary age.

Chapter Eleven

Bart Griffin was one of those nondescript kids you'd never remember in a million years. He was so unlike Tod Yaeger and Quin Jefferson that it was difficult for a moment to connect him at all. He was sort of medium. Medium scrawny, medium tall, medium brown hair, medium faded jeans, medium grey eyes, medium disinterested in what he was doing, which was trying to explain to a mother that scuba diving lessons for her daughter would not result in her being dined on by a shark. He was patient. He spoke in a monotone. He covered his mouth when he yawned. One might be moved to surmise that at Pacific Marine and Scuba Bart Griffin had not found his niche. For so young a man he gave the peculiar impression of playing out the string at the end of a dismal season.

I waited around poking at bits of gear which meant nothing to me and finally he'd finished with the lady and had gone up to the front of the store where he stood staring out into the street. He was whistling tunelessly. He just didn't give a shit.

I walked over and told him I'd been looking for him. A momentary look of total terror flickered across the grey eyes: maybe it was my imagination. I sort of hoped it was because it wasn't a pretty sight. What could scare somebody so deeply, so quickly? Did I look like a narc? Was it something else?

'You found me, I guess.' He wasn't even sure about that which meant this was a kid who wasn't sure about much. He didn't even ask who I was but I told him.

'Your sister came to me to help find your father. He's disappeared and she's worried. Then it turned out that neither she or your mother knew where you were either . . . and I just happened to find you first.' He didn't ask me how I'd found him. Apparently he just didn't care. 'I think they'd like to know just why you went into hiding.' I determined to wait him out.

He thought about that for awhile. He was growing a moustache which was too light a shade to show up until you took a hard look. He couldn't seem to force himself to make an impression. 'What do you mean I went into hiding? What's that supposed to mean, anyway? You call this hiding? Makes me sound like a criminal. Or is that still the way they look at me? The big drug runner?' The words sounded sarcastic but not when he spoke them. They were quite uninflected. 'I work. I got a job. I got a crummy little apartment. I'm in the phone book. How's that hiding?' He had me there. 'You just got conned by Sue and mother. They like to make mountains out of molehills. Maybe all women do. I don't. Honestly, I don't care. They say I'm in hiding or missing when the truth is they just didn't bother to look for me.' He shrugged. 'Who cares? You're wasting your time, I think – '

'There's still the matter of your father,' I said.

'Oh, really?'

'He's disappeared from the boat where he's been living.'

'Gimme a break.'

'What do you mean, Bart?'

'Silas is no more missing than I am. He's got his problems but being missing isn't one of them. I can tell you where to find him any time you want.' He leaned back against a stack of icechests and cupped his chin in one hand. I might as well not have been there.

I reminded him that I was. 'So? Where is he?'

'Oh, Silas, right? Well, he's going with this girl, cute girl, actually . . . Too good for him, I suppose. No, I take that back. I'm out of my judgmental phase.' That thought made him smile for the first time and he suddenly looked like a different man. The grey eyes took on a lustre, the sallow cheeks seemed to fill up and colour. 'Not that I don't backslide from time to time.' He looked me in the eye for the first time and I smiled back.

'Backsliding. It's easy to do.'

'This girl really is young enough to be his daughter. I think she's an actress or something. Commercials, maybe. I keep thinking I recognized her from somewhere. Her name's Rhonda Park.'

'You've seen her, then?'

'Yeah, I've run into them together a few times. I think they live down in Venice. At least they were Venice bars where I saw them. One Mexican cantina joint right on the beach. Saw 'em rollerskating once. Can you believe it? Silas rollerskating? But then, he's gone through some changes. Rhonda seemed okay, sort of aggressive and cute. She's not exactly my idea of a stepmother. But then Shirley is not exactly my idea of a mother. For that matter, Silas is no big success as a father. But I figure, what the hell? Everybody's alone. Nobody's ever gotten out alive.' Bart was coming to teenage profundities a little late in life. But I suppose that's better than never passing through that stage at all. It all meant Jean Paul Sartre and black turtlenecks and Juliette Greco recordings.

'Well, you're certainly right there,' I said. 'But it's

nice to hear you sound a little conciliatory about Silas. The trouble between you and your father, was that all because of the problem with Withers's boat?'

He cocked his head and gave me a sideways look, a hint of the smile still clinging to his medium plain, medium colourless mouth. 'You want me to tell you about my father? Okay, I think maybe I will. Gonna cost you a cup of coffee, friend.'

He went to the back of the store and spoke with a guy in a plaid jacket who was sitting in the office watching television. The boss. Must have been a slow day. Nobody had come in since the scuba lady had left. Griffin came back and led the way out onto Wilshire. There were a million places to get coffee. He picked a pancake house. We went inside. Turned out he wanted some blueberry pancakes, sausage, and whipped butter with his coffee. It was fine with me. The kid was a good investment. He'd already told me where Silas was and who he was with.

I watched him tuck into the pancakes. I had another chance right then to cut myself out of the rest of the game. I could go find Silas, tell him his daughter was worried. He could call her, put her mind at ease, and I was out of it. Why people were killing people and using his yacht as the venue wasn't my problem. Buy the kid his pancakes, get the hell out of their lives. But I didn't do that. I wanted to hear what young Bart had to say about life with father.

He looked up from the first half of his stack of cakes and drained off his coffee, waved to the waitress and pointed at his cup. He watched her pour, then added four teaspoons of sugar.

'The trouble between my father and me. Okay. Let's see. It didn't *begin*. It was always there. Just there. In Silas's mind we were all extensions of him. It was his ego, I suppose – he had to be the centre, he had to control. It was like putting a brand on all of us, each of us. My mother, my sister, and me. I mean, we're talking a kind of psychosis here – like he wanted us all to have the same initials. No shit! So he could stamp *SG* on everything. My name, for instance. It's Samuel. Samuel Barrett Griffin. But when I got wise to the old man, which was about ten years ago, I made it Bart. Man, he hated that but I ran away a couple of times and generally made a real pain in the ass of myself and he finally gave in. You know, sometimes I think he married Shirley because her name started with an "*S*". I mean we're talking egomaniac here.' Bart frowned and took another crack at the cakes. 'But I guess he's had some of the starch taken out of him in the last year or two.'

I watched him eat for a while and thought about Silas's egomania and all the 'S's. Silas, Sam, Susie, and Shirley. Weird.

Rhonda Park. Must have changed his mind about things. She gets new luggage.

Chapter Twelve

I could still smell the syrup and the blueberry cakes but the plate had been cleared away. I expected him to have a nice dessert but he surprised me and we sat drinking coffee together. Once he'd begun talking about his father he didn't seem to want to stop. I had the feeling he'd thought about things for a long time but hadn't really told anyone. He lit a cigarette and slurped some coffee and looked out the window. That particular stretch of Wilshire wasn't all that inspiring but he wasn't looking at Wilshire. He was looking at his father's life, his own life, trying to see the point.

'Silas changed a whole lot about the time I ran into all that trouble on Withers's boat. Things weren't going too well for him just then but I didn't know anything about it. I had my own thing to worry about, y'know? The shit really hit the fan and the Coast Guard and the cops and everybody seemed to think we were about on a par with the Manson Family. I couldn't figure it out – what was such a big deal? And Silas popped his cork. But it wasn't just me . . . and all Shirley could worry about was whether or not Tod was queer – I mean it really was looney tunes. It was easy for Silas to jump in and get pissed off at me. I guess he could use me to focus all his anger and his frustrations and disappointments and God only knows what else. It was a mess.'

I was beginning to think that Bart might be the one in the family with the best head on his shoulders. He'd gotten out and maybe he was better off for it. He'd had time to think rather than just bat the subject around with the rest of them.

'Sad part of it all was that Silas really should have been on top of the world. He'd made more money than he'd ever dreamed of. The video games had gone through the roof and the personal computer thing was just coming over the horizon and he was a first rate software designer. The whole industry was going nuts, the shakeout hadn't hit yet so there was a new company on every block. Any of them would have been delighted to get a piece of Silas Griffin. And then things started going wrong, flying apart . . . and my little disaster with Tod was just one of them.

'I can remember Silas going to trade shows and he'd meet these company presidents who weren't old enough to vote and, man, it blew his mind. These kids were making millions and it didn't look like it was ever going to stop. He was past forty-five but he was young, y'know? But he was an old man in this business and it threw him. So he gave a lot of his money to a financial advisor and told the guy to make him rich, really rich . . . and of course the guy picked the wrong company, bought a huge interest in it, and it went belly-up in a matter of six months or so. Like the *Titanic*, only there weren't any survivors. Silas lost a bundle and that scared him even more than all those kids cleaning up. He'd tried and he'd backed the wrong kid! So, he began hitting the bottle and chasing girls my age, anything to get his youth back, I guess.' Bart looked at me quickly, as if to check my reaction to the story. I nodded glumly, asked him to go on.

'Well, then things began to come apart with Shirley and I'm not saying I blame her. Silas got pretty impossible. Shirley's pretty loyal, really. Up tight, very worried about getting older herself, very determined not to get left at the gate by some jerk she'd given the best years of her life. Not exactly a new story. And she had a point, she'd helped put him through grad school, the works. Now it looked like he was cracking up and she made a move to secure herself. She filed for divorce and made sure she came out with everything she needed to keep herself afloat. Silas didn't seem to give much of a damn. The fight had just gone out of him. He was flapping around like a deflated balloon. Went off to live on the *Baja Dream*. Didn't work much. He still had royalties from the video games but there were new games every week and they weren't his. Shirley thought it was all an act, poor mouth she called it, but it was for real. Listen, he and I had bad problems but I was trying to get myself straightened out and I had some talks with him on the boat and I'll tell you the truth, I felt sorry for him. And there wasn't a damn thing I could do . . .'

I said: 'But why did your arrest really blow the top off things for him? I mean, you were found innocent.'

Bart shook his head sadly, forgetting I was even there. 'I think in his screwed up state of mind, he saw Tod and me making some big scores and we were just kids, just like those computer kids he was running into. Tod and I had money to burn and he hated that. He saw himself slipping backwards and the kids getting ahead of him. Pretty tough on a basically macho guy. Then Tod bought that marina – well, that was the last straw. He just saw red. Tod had bought the marina where Silas kept his boat! Real tough for the old boy to swallow.' He chuckled to himself. 'Tod being a fag and all didn't help, I guess.'

I said: 'Then you're admitting to me that you and Tod were running dope, right?'

Bart narrowed his eyes and his voice suddenly filled again with suspicion. The terror wasn't there but I'd identified its source. He really did think I might be a narc. 'I didn't admit anything. Tod and I made some investments, that's all. Who the hell are you, anyway? What's the point of all this?'

'I told you. I'm a friend of your sister's. I teach one of her courses at Cal State. I'm not out to get anybody. I just wanted to find her father. You've been a big help, Bart.'

He was looking at me more closely, like a man straining to read a newspaper from across the table.

'Sue has always had a thing for older guys. Electra Complex, y'know? Wants to screw her father and kill her mother.'

'It's funny. Your mother went out of her way to tell me about her penchant for older men. Why do you think she'd do that?'

'I dunno,' he shrugged. 'Because it's true. Sue was always on Silas's side, daddy's little girl. He couldn't do anything wrong. You know how it goes.'

'Who are all these older men in her life?'

'I only know about the one, actually. I didn't try to keep tabs on Sue's life. Our value systems are not exactly the same. But there was this one guy. A Mexican. But it was over a year ago. A good long year, anyway. He worked for a gallery or a museum or something in Mexico City. She had a big crush on him and it was obvious she was sleeping with him. Big deal. So what? Who cares?'

'His name wasn't Freddie Sanchez, by any chance?'

'Yeah, Sanchez. That's the guy.' He was bored by the whole subject, probably figuring that I was just another older guy hot for his little sister. 'You know him or something?'

98

'No, I didn't know him. But he was murdered the other day. In San Amaro.'

'You don't say?' He didn't seem unduly concerned. He was drifting away from me again, returning to his earlier form.

'Sue and I found his body.'

'Ouch. That must have shaken her up –'

'We found him dead on the *Baja Dream*.'

Chapter Thirteen

I sat there like a statue in the park, frozen in place by Bart's revelation of Susie's love affair with the late Frederico Sanchez. The questions flew up like pigeons in the path of a kicker. What was her number, anyway? Why lie to me? And, worse for her, to the cops? Phil Redding hated having citizens give him the bird. Older men, older men, that had been a constant refrain about Susie . . . and now the other shoe had dropped.

Bart shook his head, doubtless unaware of my concern. He was thinking about himself again, now that he'd unburdened himself about Silas and Shirley.

'Boy, that musta been rough on Sue. She was there when you found him? Oh, wow. What can I say?' I tuned out on the generational clichés and when they were done I told him about that night, the body in the utility closet, the sailcloth wrapping, the icons.

'This is all news to you?' I must have sounded more than a little unbelieving.

'Look, I don't read the papers much, particularly not the dear old *News-Hour*. The LA *Times* probably didn't give it much of a play . . . look, I'm getting into Tibetan Buddhism, okay? I spend most of my time reading that. The stuff I could tell you – '

'Spare me,' I said. 'I'm still wrestling with being born a Presbyterian. What do you know about icons?'

He gave me a blank look. 'Sort of religious paintings, aren't they? Greek or something. Maybe Sanchez had something to do with them.' He shrugged. 'What did Sue do when she saw him?'

'Not much. She didn't tell me she knew him, for one thing. That doesn't figure – '

He smiled inwardly, as if remembering his sister from childhood. 'Sure, it figures. Sue's always had a life of her own going on inside herself, full of secrets, not wanting people to know what she's thinking or doing. Secrets have always been a big deal to her – I don't think it means anything serious about her, just a personality trait. She probably figured Sanchez was her secret and she wanted to keep it that way . . . Frankly, I don't think it was much of a secret. Ever. Not if I knew about it.'

I walked him back across the street to Pacific Marine and Scuba. I shook his hand. He wasn't a bad kid. He nodded and slapped me on the back, like a man wishing a luckless friend good luck. I wondered if he'd noticed my concern over Susie and Sanchez. He struck me as reasonably observant.

I went back to the VW and turned around, drove back toward the ocean, and turned north. What kind of a game was Susie playing? And who else was in on it? Did her mother know about Sanchez? If so they were both jerking my chain and I hated that. I wasn't even getting paid! Maybe Levine was right. Loser. Why would Susie stay quiet, looking down at the corpse of a man who had been her lover? The immediate response anyone would have to her behaviour, I guess, would be to assume that she had some involvement in his death. But if she did, why would she let me go to the boat at all? Of course, she hadn't really wanted me to go the *Baja Dream,* had kept telling me we were wasting time. And once we were there, she'd tried to leave – she'd actually been on deck when I insisted on looking in the utility closet . . .

And if Shirley had known about Susie and Sanchez and had subsequently remained silent about the relationship, coming up with the cracked idea that the murdered man might have been a drug runner trying to steal the boat . . . if all that was true, you had to wonder if maybe Shirley was involved in murder.

Was one protecting the other, mother and daughter? But if so, which was which? It was just so messy and there was only one thing I could think of to do about it.

I found Susie at the off-campus house where she lived. It was probably a ten minute drive from her home but I suppose she'd wanted to live with the other kids and I couldn't blame her. It was an old Victorian house full of girls in various stages of undress. Nobody was shy and there sure wasn't any housemother. Things had changed a lot since I was a college boy who'd have sold his grandmother for a look at a girl in her underpants. I discussed Susie's possible whereabouts with a darkhaired girl who made me want to chew on my shoe. I sat in a downstairs parlour where girls in workout clothes and robes were watching a TV show which featured a distraught blonde woman confiding to her maid: 'If Alex is seeing Fay on the side, without Nolan's knowledge, she certainly hasn't told me.' The maid was chewing gum and said: 'Be reasonable, Countess. He'd have to be out of his mind to confide in you!' As far as I was concerned, my heart went out to Nolan who was probably a wimp who deserved whatever Fay did to him.

'Hi,' Susie said brightly from behind me. I turned

102

around and she was wearing jeans and a plaid shirt and I wished we were going to have any conversation other than the one we were going to have. She was freshly scrubbed and shining. 'Hey, you must have come up with something! Tell, tell . . .' She touched my arm.

'Yeah,' I said. 'Couple things. Let's go for a walk.'

She kind of bounced along beside me. Excited. The shadows were long and the day had produced a glorious sunset. Palms and sycamores and elms. Nice white-frame houses with green shutters. The Beav and Wally were probably inside learning another one of life's little lessons. A gentle world. The legacy of Ozzie and Harriet. But like Bart Griffin had said, nobody ever got out of it alive.

'I found your brother, for one thing,' I said.

'How in the world did you find him? Where is he?'

'I spoke to Aaron Withers in Malibu. What a piece of work he is! Anyway, he had kept tabs on Bart after the trial – don't ask me why. Withers is not the kind of man you can explain. Anyway, I went to Santa Monica where Bart works in a marine supply store. We had a long talk.'

She teased me. 'That sounds pretty ominous. How is he? Did he have a word for me or Mom? Or is that asking too much?'

'He's fine, I guess. He had a fair amount to say about the family – '

'Oh-oh.' She grinned. 'Here it comes.'

I stopped and took her arm to keep her from skipping happily away. 'Why didn't you tell me about Sanchez?'

'Tell you what?' But her face was beginning to come apart and I didn't want to look.

'Maybe you thought it was a secret, I don't know. But most secrets aren't so secret after all. He told me

103

you'd been having a love affair with Sanchez . . .' I watched her hand fly to her mouth. Her front teeth clamped down on the knuckle. 'It was very dumb to hold out on me. And a good deal worse to withold that kind of information from the police. For one thing, it makes you look very suspicious, indeed – '

'You don't think that I had anything . . . oh, you can't believe that!' And she was crying, staring wide-eyed at me, tears streaming down her pink cheeks. 'I haven't seen him in a year – ' She pulled away from me and leaned against the trunk of a palm tree.

'You'd be well-advised to tell me the truth.' I sounded cold and official which was the way I wanted to sound. 'If it becomes necessary, I can speak on your behalf to Phil Redding.'

'How did Bart even know?' She wouldn't look at me. She'd done nothing to wipe away the tears. A dog on a nearby lawn was regarding her with curiosity, just short of barking.

'I don't know. It's not important – '

'How do you know it's not important? It might be.'

'Let that take care of itself, Susie. Just give me the story of you and Sanchez.'

'Well, when I saw him dead and all wrapped up like that . . . and the smell . . . I guess I was so shocked, so sickened by the whole thing, that I went a little haywire in my mind. I didn't want to connect myself to a murder. It's that simple. And my relationship with him had been over for ages – it was neat while it lasted but it was over. So I didn't see the point . . . I didn't want to be connected with his murder because I'm not connected with his murder. Everybody would have jumped to crazy conclusions – just like you did! I knew that would happen if I said anything! And we'd been very discreet . . .' She finally took a tissue from her pocket and dabbed at her face.

'Did your mother lie for you, too? Or didn't she know?'

She swallowed and blew her nose. 'She found out about Freddie and me about the time it was ending. By accident, she saw us and confronted me with her assumptions and I admitted it. When she saw that I hadn't told anyone about my affair with Sanchez she picked up on it, went along. Later she told me I might as well keep quiet about it. She said it would just confuse the issue and interfere with the real investigation – '

'*But why was he on the Baja Dream?*' I was giving her a very stern look. She seemed to adore it. Damn.

'I don't know.'

'Well, there has to be a reason. Could he have been trying to reach you?'

'I can't imagine why. Look, we didn't stay in touch. It was over. Finished. It's a part of my life I'd like to forget.'

'How did you get involved with Freddie Sanchez in the first place?'

'He used to come up to Los Angeles and San Amaro fairly often. Business trips for the museum, he said. And a couple of years ago he joined our country club here in San Amaro. I was spending a lot of time there playing tennis and Freddie played really well. I played doubles with him a few times, he got in the habit of watching me play, offered some pointers. I was only nineteen and I was having a pretty tough time of it. Mom and dad were breaking up and I missed dad a lot . . . and along came Freddie and he liked me and he was attentive and made me feel good about myself. I suppose I viewed him as a kind of father figure to replace my dad. And when I realized he was romantically interested in me – well, it was exciting. I was being pursued by this Latin who was almost my

105

father's age . . .' She looked at me imploringly, begging me to understand and accept what was going through her mind at the time.

'Was there a Mrs Sanchez somewhere in the background?'

'No. He said he'd been divorced for years.'

'What did he ever tell you about his work?'

She shrugged. 'Just chit-chat. Nothing I remember.'

'Think hard, Susie. Did he ever talk to you about icons?'

She shook her head. 'I know nothing about them. If he ever mentioned icons it couldn't have been more than in passing. I'd remember if he'd made a point of them.' She fell into step beside me and we walked in the cool shadows, the sun slanting at us from out across the bay. From the end of the block we could see the *Baja Dream* shining like a white hope, full of promise.

'Did Freddie ever mention Aaron Withers? The guy who owned the boat Bart was on when everything hit the fan – '

'No. I truly don't remember that he ever did – '

'Withers is into icons,' I said. 'There's got to be a connection somewhere. At least there'd better be. Did you ever come across Withers at the country club?'

'I don't think so. I thought he lived in Malibu?'

'So what? Freddie Sanchez lived in Mexico City. You wouldn't forget Withers, in any case. About six-two, three hundred pounds or so, bald as a cue ball, cigar like a log – '

'No. He was never around the club when I was.'

We were walking back towards the house and you'd never know she'd been crying. I wished I felt as good about things as I should have.

'Bart also told me where your father is,' I said.

She stopped and gasped, sort of jumped up and down. 'You're kidding! Why didn't you tell me? Where is he?'

'Living down in Venice. Bart didn't give me the address – I don't think he knows. But he's seen your dad with his girlfriend, a woman named Rhonda Park. I think I'm going to run down there and maybe I can find her. If your dad isn't living with her she's bound to know where he is.'

'Great idea! Can I come?'

'I was going to suggest it.'

'Oh, it'll be so good to see him, see that he's okay!'

'I'll swing by here and pick you up in the morning.'

I watched her run up the walk to the house. The resilience of youth can seem pretty awesome when you're getting on. I went back to the car and sat for awhile thinking about Silas Griffin. Thinking about all the money he'd once had and where it all had led him.

To Venice and a woman named Rhonda Park.

She didn't even have the right initials.

Chapter Fourteen

I went back to the beach house and took a shower and wondered where this all was taking me. I didn't know and I couldn't seem to work up a premonition. I called Jan at her place but she wasn't there either. Probably at her store. I wanted to stop by with a pizza and some beer and forget about the Griffins and all their problems.

Instead, I opened a bag of chocolate goobers and called Phil Redding to see if he had turned up anything I should know about.

He growled: 'The guy from the museum in Mexico City flew in and had a look at the icons. He's been playing with them all afternoon. I'm just heading over to his hotel now for the official word. He's at the Alta Vista. You wanta come?'

'Sure.'

'His name's Pablo Juzgar. Doctor Juzgar to you. I'll meet you there.'

I put on a clean shirt and clean chinos and shiny loafers and a pretty spiffy blue blazer and went outside and got into the filthy car. Go figure.

The Alta Vista overlooked the bay and the oil rigs and the gulls and the yachts and the ant farm that was daily life. All cool tiles and palms bending in the breeze from the recessed fans and dark furniture in the Mexican style. Lots of polished wood showing.

Shirley Griffin would have felt right at home. Phil Redding was standing by the discreet little desk that didn't seem to want to admit that it took money in return for its friendship and service. He saw me coming and started toward the dim little bar with its glass wall with the palms and cacti and sprinkling, splashing fountains beyond. I followed him. We sat at a low table by the glass and pretended we were two carefree guys in Eden. I ordered a gimlet and Phil said he thought he'd have a beer, any beer, he didn't really care. The waiter bowed as if he understood precisely the gentleman's state of mind. The very best thing about the bar at the Alta Vista was the nuts. Cashews, salty and oily or dry roasted, both kinds, right on your table and you could eat them like there was no tomorrow. It was worth having to talk like you were in a library.

'So what have you been up to?' Redding asked as if he wasn't all that interested.

'Located my missing father for Susie Griffin – '

'Oh yeah? Where?'

'Down Venice way. Found the son, Bart, too – '

'What's he up to? Still running dope?'

'You know, I think he really was guilty – '

'Bravo! Quick-witted private eye finally reaches the darkest heart of the matter. Of course he was guilty. Justice is blind.'

'He's working in Santa Monica. Studying Tibetan Buddhism – '

Phil grimaced. 'Well, the only harm he's likely to do with that is bore somebody to death.' He laughed immoderately at his own wit. Sounded like a nuclear explosion in the delicate stillness of the bar. I felt as if I'd landed on another, much better planet. 'What about the father? Rich guy like that, five'll get you

109

fifty he's shacked up with Miss Venice of '74 and she's still looking pretty good.' He grinned expectantly.

'Bart says he's got a girlfriend, sure. But I'm not so sure about the money part of it. Bart said his dad's had some pretty tough times since the divorce . . . business wise, lost a lot of money. Financial manager turned out to be not so smart after all . . .'

Phil nodded. 'Let me tell you something, in case you ever get rich.' He took a long drink of Lone Star Beer and belched. 'Last year, here in San Amaro, we had fifteen percent of the richest male citizens under fifty kill themselves . . . that's three out of twenty guys, all country club types, all with yachts, just like your Silas Griffin. Three out of twenty. And why? I'll tell you why. Financial managers. Don't know their ass, they glom on to some guy's money, tell him how they're gonna shelter this and double that and leverage the other thing and the poor dumb mark who's made his money writing screenplays or getting lucky with some scientific doodad, he doesn't know a thing either, and the first thing you know the bloody hole was dry, the cattle froze to death in a Texas blizzard, and the shopping centre never got built after all . . . and we got a forty-five year old guy who had a few million right up until yesterday putting a .357 Magnum in his mouth and blowing his brains halfway to Marin County. Financial managers – they oughta lock the bastards up.' He spoke like a man who'd once lost $500 to a sharpie.

Dr. Pablo Juzgar arrived about ten minutes after Phil had relieved himself of his thoughts regarding financial wizards. He was tall and rounded and smooth and well-dressed and carried a soft leather piece of carry-on luggage. He was looking at his watch as he sat down. He was dark, and had a smooth bald head with long grey strands slicked back above his ears.

Gold ring on his little finger, gold wristwatch thin as a quarter. Tailored half to death. He ordered a Perrier, plain, no lime, and told Phil that he'd left the icons in the hotel safe.

'So, are they the real thing?'

'In my opinion, yes. I am not an expert in icons, *per se*, but I am not uninformed in the field. I would say they are excellent small pieces. Ultimately they will have to be tested scientifically, as a matter of course. But, yes, they are real.' He lit a cigarette with a gold lighter which clicked solidly, like the door of a very tiny Rolls Royce.

'And how,' Phil said, working on a second Lone Star, 'would you say they came to be at the scene of Mr Sanchez's murder – '

His lips curled down in a perfect moue. 'How am I to say? I have conducted no investigation, after all. I have only my own subjective thoughts . . .'

'Well, I am investigating, Dr Juzgar, and I'm just wondering what your own thoughts might be. Sanchez was an employee of your museum, you were his boss, the head curator. Just share your subjective thoughts – '

'Well, I am running late. I mustn't miss my plane from LAX. My driver should be here by now . . . ah, Mr Sanchez, yes, well . . . there's always the danger of a certain amount of chicanery in our profession. The temptations are there, the opportunities present themselves. The art world attracts men who are – frankly – unscrupulous. More often than not, they are readily identifiable and can be avoided. But sometimes . . .' He shrugged.

'What kind of scam usually occurs?' Phil asked.

'The best, most potentially successful schemes are those involving, first, longtime and trusted employees, and second, the switching of small, relatively unimposing works of art which, in fact, may not even be on exhibit most of the time. An expert curator has access to the storage rooms, what he does is not likely to be closely questioned. A very small work, one of many hundred in storage, may be switched with a good copy of it, and it might be literally a century before the fake is identified . . . if indeed it is ever identified. It might well survive forever as a work of art when in fact it was painted last month by a struggling artist needing money for food.' He tapped his watch and craned to look behind him into the lobby.

I said: 'You mean, once the curator is on the take, and once the switch is made, there is virtually no way of catching the culprits – '

'More or less. Say the switch is somehow discovered. Try proving how it was accomplished . . . and when. Next to impossible. No, you have to apprehend someone virtually in the act of copying, stealing, or buying the work in question. Once the mission is accomplished, so to speak, it's much more difficult. My own doubts about – ah,' he leaped to his feet. 'My driver, thank God.' He shook hands with both of us and asked to be kept informed. Redding assured him he would, adding that he might be required to return. Juzgar nodded, as if to say, once I'm on that plane you may do your best to get me back . . .

'Your own doubts about Sanchez?' I asked.

He looked at me sharply. 'There has been a theory that we are being victimised, have been victimised for some time, by a thievery operation. No proof, but a couple of forgeries have been found among pieces of pottery, a couple among the lesser paintings. No guilt attaching to anyone. But, now, you can see how my mind must be working.' He was sweeping along to the lobby, taller than either of us. We were following. He had that air of control which makes everyone else

112

put his needs first. 'I find that one of my curators has been murdered and he seems to have three icons – genuine – with him. Now we must discover if the icons belonged to us and if they did, have they been replaced with fakes or are we just missing three icons. Now, again, I must be off.'

We watched the limo pull away.

Phil sighed. '*Vaya con dios,* jerk.'

We turned around and went back into the bar and I fell hungrily on the cashews. Phil ordered another round and said: 'Everybody's got a problem, everybody's got a story. Poor Sanchez, trying to make a buck. Peddling icons. Maybe. Who the hell knows?'

I thought that maybe I did. I kept seeing the little icons in Aaron Withers's home and thinking he might be capable of any damn craziness.

Or so it seemed.

Chapter Fifteen

Time is a Great Teacher
But Unfortunately it Kills all its Pupils.
— Berlioz

Lime green lettering on a yellow tee-shirt. Breasts very jaunty today, as well, evidence of a general state of high spirits which I wasn't quite able to share. I did my best, however, and I didn't have to talk much.

'You want the top down?' I said.

'Sure, why not?' She reached into her Yo-Yo Ma bag and took out a bandanna which she tied around her blonde hair. Very fetching.

'Good thing,' I said. 'Top doesn't come up, anyway.'

We curved down the hairpins to the highway and headed south. She had a grin like the original free spirit, all California girl. That morning she looked like her mother's daughter, all right. She had that California girl's way of grinning into the sun and the wind, daring it, showing she could take it. The free ends of her hair whipped in the wind. She made me feel twenty-five and rich. They're dangerous, the way they make you believe all the lies you tell yourself before hope begins to get shot away in the battle.

We hit Malibu and she said she felt like a cheeseburger.

I'm a pretty witty guy when I'm in full cry. I told her that was weird, she sure didn't look like a cheeseburger. She told me I was crazy.

We stopped and ate and I pretended I was Jim Rockford and everything was going to turn out all right. It was a perfect case for Jimbo because he never seemed to get paid either. We baked in the sun and felt the sweat drying and smelled the salt and the sand and looked out to sea. Sometimes they say you can see the whales sounding out there. I never have, but I believe them. She told me I was awfully nice to go to all this trouble and I said that's the kind of guy I am. She looked at me for a long time while I watched the people on the beach. I felt her eyes on me the way George Raft would have felt the searchlight in an old prison break flick. I wanted her to watch me. I wanted her to want to watch me. The thing was, I was probably about halfway there if I wanted to have her. She had the predilection for older guys and I sure as hell qualified. And we got along. And I wondered just how safe, and I thought of Sanchez wrapped up in his sailcloth shroud.

Finally I looked back into her eyes and said: 'Stop watching me, you rude girl.'

'No,' she said.

The rest of the way to Venice was just urban sprawl and I turned the radio on and we listened to Boy George, Eurythmics and Tina Turner and the sun beat down and the wind blew and I kept wondering what she'd think when her illusions about her rich father got blown to hell. Rich is one of those things that some people don't seem to think is important until they find out what not-rich is like. Then they wind up talking to themselves and eating rocks off the street. Like, crazy. Maybe her feelings for her father didn't have anything to do with money. I hoped they didn't. I hoped they had to do with loving him. Ever hopeful. Ought to be tatooed on my chest.

We hit Venice and stopped at a drugstore and I scrounged up a telephone book and we found Rhonda Park. Information didn't have a Silas Griffin which wasn't much of a surprise. Too soon. I jotted down Park's address and got directions from the kid standing behind the counter.

She lived down by the beach in a stucco eight-plex but there was nobody home. The yard was more sand than grass but it wasn't a bad building. Beach people cared about the beach, bottom line, and weren't picky about snazzy digs.

'Let's check out some of the joints Bart told me about,' I said. 'They'll be open now. We can walk.'

We headed up the sandy sidewalk toward a big pink building with pink stucco pillars holding up the balcony, which had a bit of a sag to it. It looked bullet scarred and I expected a bandido to come around the corner stepping on his moustache, yelling *gringo! gringo!*, and there'd be Pike Bishop and the Wild Bunch heading for the last hurrah. Instead, the roller-skaters went whisking along listening to their pocket stereos and the breakers were washing in on the beach and little kids were pulling with sticky hands on their mothers' shorts.

'Did I ever tell you about my uncle?' I asked.

'No.'

'He did this incredible trick. He could walk down any street in America and turn into a bar – '

'That,' she giggled, 'is worse than the cheeseburger.'

'I got a million of 'em. Just don't ever ask me to call you a cab. Heh, heh.'

Incredibly enough, she took my hand.

Maybe it was like helping a very old chap across the street. And maybe not.

We stopped at a bar which looked like the kind of place a Rhonda Park might hang out. It was dark and cool after the afternoon sun. We sat on high stools beneath a neon depiction of *el toro* and the matador giving each other dirty looks. I asked the bartender questions and it was a slow afternoon and we both wondered if the Rams' wide-receivers had the speed they needed. To us it looked like Joe Montana was gonna take the Forty-Niners all the way. And by that time we were old pals exchanging bookies' numbers and I asked him about Rhonda Park.

'Hey, man . . .' he said, palms outstretched. 'I can't talk about my customers. You know Rhonda?'

'Not exactly.' I smiled. Susie smiled. We all smiled. I couldn't remember when I'd last had so much fun. 'This is crazy but I'm with William Morris, we got a client who's shooting a commercial up in Malibu and it turns out the guy's seen this Rhonda Park in commercials and he springs it on us today – he's got to have her in the shoot. Imagine my surprise. Telephone calls and agents sobbing and time a-wasting, y'know? Anyway, we found out she lives down here but we just checked, nobody home. Hell, I thought she might be on the beach or maybe somebody had seen her . . .' I was running out of gas but Rockford would have given me a C+ for the story. Better than nothing.

He looked at me appraisingly, cupping his chin in the palm of his hand, grinning. Then he must have figured what the hell, who cares?

'Yeah,' he said, 'the funny thing is, I saw her an

117

hour or so ago. She stopped in for cigarettes. Had her beach towel with the guy riding the polo pony on it. She lies in the sun, keeps that body the colour of *café au lait*, y'know? *Olé!*'

He told us the general direction she'd gone and described her. I got the picture. She wouldn't be hard to find.

The bartender had been right about everything.

Her colour was like the best tasting coffee of your life. Made you want to lick the spoon. Her blonde hair was cut very short and lay in flat little daggers across her forehead. Her eyes were big as saucers and ocean blue. Her bathing suit looked like somebody had gone to lunch halfway through making it and never came back. She was short and perky even while lying down. Her beach towel had a guy on a polo pony, leaning over about to hit her in the kneecap with his mallet. She blinked and opened her eyes when my shadow fell across her face.

'Silas Griffin,' I said.

She blinked some more and shielded her eyes.

'We're looking for Silas Griffin, Miss Park. Do you think maybe you could help us find him?'

She was squirming around trying to sit up and her breasts reminded me of two tennis balls trying to roll away. She shook her head. 'Sleeping,' she murmured. She stood up and she was so cute that I didn't know whether to adopt her or molest her. 'Look, I don't know you . . . why should I tell you anything? Name, rank, and serial number, that's my motto.' She grinned and leaned over and began to gather her sun lotion and the paperback she'd been reading, pitching them into a beachbag with a drawstring.

'Silas's son told us where to find you,' I said. Susie

118

was watching her intently. I had the feeling that she was analyzing Rhonda Park's appeal and relating it to the needs of her father. She had that light in her eye and I knew she was imagining all sorts of things, including her father and Rhonda Park in bed. I turned and introduced Susie, laid out my own name, and explained that we'd just been worried because Silas had dropped out of sight.

'I don't mean to be rude,' she said, 'but Silas pretty much has the right to see and talk to whomever he wants, right? I mean, if he wanted to see you, he'd know how to get hold of you. So I'm not so sure I should just run off at the mouth about how to get to him yourselves.' She yanked the drawstring and started across the sand.

We followed along and I kept talking, trying to explain what awfully decent folks we were. She kept nodding and we wound up at her apartment.

'You might at least tell me how he is,' Susie said.

'He's all right. He's been pretty jumpy about things, but he's okay. Getting better.' She opened the door, gave a halfhearted look in our direction, and invited us in. The room was dim and cool, the airconditioner whirring in a window, the blinds drawn against the sun reflecting off the beach.

'Was he sick?' Susie asked. 'Better from what?'

'Well, of course he was sick!' Rhonda was exasperated, already saying more than she intended. But she was so perky and talkative and energetic she couldn't quite stop the flow of conversation. 'I mean, listen, your daddy's an alcoholic. That's sick. When we met it was ugly, he made a pass at me in a bar not far from here and then he fainted – right in the booth! I thought he was dead! But he came to and all the starch was out of him, if you know what I mean. He was a different guy all of a sudden and while he got to

119

feeling a little better we started talking. He didn't even remember the pass he'd made but apologised like mad! And I really liked him a lot. So we went out for burgers that night, about three in the morning, and he asked if he could call me again for a real dinner . . . and that's how we got started. Now he's doing everything he can to lick this problem he has with booze . . .' She batted the huge blue eyes, thinking where her remarks might be carrying her. 'And maybe it's not so good to have your daughter just drop in by surprise. Maybe,' she brightened, wanting to hold out some hope, 'he wants to be all better before he contacts you. Doesn't that sound nice? Reasonable?' I knew where I'd seen her before. She'd been a softball player on a diet beer commercial. Cuddly, was the word. Griffin might be a boozer but his luck hadn't been all bad.

'Anyway,' Rhonda went on, 'he's stopped drinking and he's working like mad designing some of his new thingamajigs, the computer and video games. I guess that's what they are. The fact is, I don't really get a lot of what he talks about. But he had a bad time with all that, too. He blames the drinking on his marriage to Shirley – sorry, honey, but he does. He wants to make a fresh start without her. But that doesn't mean he's down on you, honey. And I think he'd have told me, y'know? And it's been tough on him watching all the young kids making so much money in his business . . .'

She bit her lip, as if she'd gone too far toward revealing what was private between her and Griffin.

'So, why don't you just wait until he gets in touch?' Rhonda had decided that she knew best and surely we'd see the light, too. 'I'm telling you he's fine, the best he's been in a long time. There's nothing to worry about – '

'Miss Park,' I interrupted, 'there's more to this

story than meets the eye. There was a murder on Mr
Griffin's yacht recently. We *need* to talk to him. It
would be better if we got to him before the police do.'
You always say things like that in such situations. It's
a clincher. Everybody always thinks it would be better
if damn near anyone got to somebody before the
police. Lesson there somewhere.

'A murder?' she asked, half-swallowing the
question.

'A murder.'

'Gosh.'

'To put it mildly.'

'Maybe that's all the more reason I shouldn't tell
you anymore – '

'Ah. Well, Miss Park,' I said, 'I have a thought. It
might satisfy your code of honour and it might also
enable Miss Griffin to see her father. Why don't you
just call him and ask if he's willing to see Susie. If he
is, great, we'll go see him. If not, perhaps he'd talk
with her on the telephone or simply give you a message
to pass on. Last thing we want to do is bug him – it's
a matter of letting him know there's concern at Susie's
end of things.'

She mulled that over for a bit and couldn't find
the treachery which would undo her good intentions.
Telling us to wait she went into the bedroom and re-
emerged ten minutes later.

She was smiling brightly, just like a toothpaste girl
which I think she had also been.

'He said okay,' Susie breathed.

Rhonda nodded. 'He said it was fine with him.' She
looked greatly relieved to give us good news. She also
gave us the address.

At the doorway I said: 'Are you coming with?'

But no, she had an audition.

'Laxative,' she said, making a cute, perky face.

Chapter Sixteen

Silas Griffin lived in a loft, the second floor of a warehouse, about six blocks from Rhonda Park's apartment. The old brick building looked as if it had started life as a firehouse, been converted to storage, and then been sort of forgotten about. The doors to the downstairs were locked and the windows were grimy. Shapes, boxes and packing crates loomed inside. A stairway led up the outside of the building to the second floor. The block was rundown and grey with the constant beating of the ocean breeze and its salt. The shrubs were gnarled and stunted and even the heat and the sunshine didn't give it a very lively look.

'Well, Susie,' I said, 'he's just up the stairs.'

'You really did find him for me, didn't you? I don't know what to say – '

'Let's go say hello.'

'Right,' she gulped and I followed her up the stairs.

Silas Griffin opened the door, took a long look at his daughter, and then took her by the shoulders and shook her slowly, appreciatively. 'Muffin,' he said.

'Daddy! You're all right!'

She threw herself into his arms and I didn't know where to look. He caught my eye over her shoulder and winked, man to man.

He cooed something into her ear and she sniffled

122

and finally we went inside. Silas Griffin looked every minute of his age and I'd have guessed he was past fifty. He was a short stocky man who'd developed a drinker's little pot and the thin, weak-looking arms that so often are part of the syndrome. His nose was small and pointed, his hair greying and sandy and combed straight back, and his voice sounded cracked, the product of a million Lucky Strikes. His voice was deep and thick and nasal, like a great baseball announcer's. When he spoke you could almost hear the crack of the bat, back in the days when they had real baseball announcers. Broken veins had splayed out across his cheeks, beneath his eyes and reaching around toward his ears. His light blue eyes had a sparkle, however, and I figured that maybe the cure had begun to take effect. He was wearing an Hawaiian sport shirt and lightblue denim baggies and hush puppies. It was hard to imagine a living creature less like the computer and video whiz kids he'd figured were passing him by. It was also just a little tough figuring out what Rhonda Park saw when she took a good hard look at him. Still, maybe she loved strays and the last Christmas tree on the lot and Silas Griffin. Maybe she had a feel for his future. Maybe she knew he wasn't done yet.

The loft had been fixed up with some big couches in one end, some wall hangings, some pots full of hanging ferns, a stereo system, a huge Indian rug, low coffee tables, gunky lamps. It was amazingly comfortable-looking and I had the feeling that they represented Rhonda's contribution to the decor. The other, larger, end of the loft sure as hell didn't.

There must have been ten television monitors and half as many keyboards and printers and racks of programs and mazes of wire and stuff I couldn't even put names to. There was a bench, stools, a draftsman's table, endless cartons of stuff, notebooks, hanging lamps and goosenecked lamps and clamp-on thingumies and . . . I looked away in an attempt to save my sanity. If he couldn't start World War III from that end of the loft I had to believe he just wasn't trying.

Griffin had led us to the couches and Susie was explaining who I was and what I was doing with her. Griffin was nodding. When she was done he looked around and said: 'I'm on the wagon, folks. Don't keep spirits in the joint anymore. But help yourself to diet soda or Coke or whatever else you can find in the fridge. Susie, would you do the honours? Make mine Sprite.' Susie bounced up and I said a Sprite would be fine with me and she went off happily, clattering icecubes and popping cans, while Griffin and I made the smallest of possible talk. When she came back, she asked him why he'd disappeared. She said she had begun to think he was really missing or wandering injured from an accident, something dire.

Griffin laughed into his Sprite. 'Nothing dire, Muffin. I wasn't even missing. Not in any sense of the word. I just met Rhonda a few months back and we hit off like a house on fire – she's a wonder, that girl. I hope you liked her, Muffy. Anyway, we got pretty close to one another and I got to thinking that I'd like to be a lot closer, mile-wise, that is. Besides living on the boat was getting to me. Cramped, claustrophobia, y'know? If I was gonna get back to work – I mean, really get back to work – on the computer designs and programs again I knew I'd need more space. I looked around and, voilà, we found this place. Rhonda knew the realtor and I followed her lead, moved in. She fixed it up nice, right? And I've been getting down to brass tacks.' He nodded toward the mountains of gear at the other end of the loft.

'But why didn't you tell me you were leaving the boat? How could we know where you'd gone?' Susie couldn't help herself. She wanted an explanation now that the reunion had been effected. She wanted to know what the hell was going on and what all this Rhonda Park hooha really meant.

'Look, Muffin, you've got to remember that I'm a grown-up. I've got my own life to live. I was trying to get off the booze once and for all and Rhonda was a part of it, moving out and into a new environment was part of it. I knew for sure that Shirley didn't give a damn where I was. And Bart – well, you know how Bart and I were getting along. Oh, the booze had a lot to do with it, I was real hard on the kid, I guess.'

'But what about me, Daddy? Why didn't you tell me?'

'Honey, I intended to tell you – you were the only one I even thought of telling. Believe me. But you know how I am when it comes to time . . . I moved and I got to thinking about working again, really getting back into it. And,' he beamed out of that ruined face, 'I had some ideas! So I set to work . . . and, forgive me, I just didn't get around to calling. *Mea culpa.*' He placed his hands over his heart, asking to be absolved. 'And besides, the last thing I expected was to have you come after me with detectives!'

'You're important to me!' she exclaimed.

I explained that, indeed, I was not a detective but acting simply as Susie's friend. 'She needed some help, Mr Griffin. I was handy.'

Susie got very serious and slid forward on the couch facing her father. 'Dad,' she said, 'there was a murder on your boat. A murder on the *Baja Dream*!' Her voice was trembling and I figured I knew why. Still, she couldn't duck the issue.

Griffin nodded slowly. 'Yes. Rhonda told me. I

don't read the papers much and Rhonda's into fitness and auditions and the Hollywood Reporter, that kind of stuff. She heard it from a friend who recognised my name.' He shook his head. 'Hell of a thing. Why my boat? Why not somebody else's boat? Seems like I've had enough problems lately.'

I said: 'The murdered man, Freddie Sanchez – did you know him? Is there anything to connect him to you?'

Susie got a little tighter, if that was possible.

Griffin shrugged. 'Never heard of him. Look, I know I should have contacted the police, but I guess I figured I couldn't help them with their investigation, so why get involved? If they wanted me I just never thought they'd have any trouble finding me. Hell, I knew where I was! I wasn't hiding . . . What a mess.' He took a long drink of the Sprite and stared into the glass. He wanted a real drink but wasn't going to have one. 'Obviously someone was using my boat in my absence. Someone who knew I wouldn't be back right away. I've thought and thought but I don't have any idea.'

'What about the icons?' I asked.

'What about what icons?' He looked awfully blank like a man thinking hard about something else.

'There were icons found on board with Sanchez's body. Does that mean anything to you?'

'Christ, no! What would I know about icons? I'm a scientist, a computer man, not an art expert. I'm not even sure what an icon is – a statue or something?'

I told him what an icon was. 'The way it looks right now – and I'm just winging this – is that Sanchez – who was an art curator – stole them from the museum in Mexico City where he worked. He'd substitute forgeries for them. Three of them were found on the *Baja Dream* along with his body.'

Griffin jumped to his feet and slammed a balled up fist into his palm. 'Why the hell was it my boat? Are you telling me I'm going to have trouble because of this? Talk about an innocent bystander!' He paced around the couch and his face was getting redder, which wasn't easy.

'I don't know that you're going to have any trouble,' I said. 'That's pretty much up to the police and however they conduct their investigations. As you say, there had to be someone who knew you wouldn't be back using the boat right away. How about Tod Yaeger? He strikes me as a fairly creepy specimen. Did you tell him you were taking an apartment here in Venice? I mean, you might have – notifying that the boat would be empty and he might take a little extra care, checking it out – '

'Creepy specimen! You're much too kind, my friend. He's a rotten son-of-a-bitch if ever there was one. Pervert! He damn near got my son locked away in a cell for five years – I wouldn't tell the bastard if he was on fire!'

Griffin stalked off to get himself another can of soda and I stretched my legs, poking around the room. There was a fly buzzing at the window and when I got up close it turned out to be a bee. I took a swipe at it and got a bit of a shock.

Looking out the window I saw a familiar face across the street.

Quin Jefferson was standing in a doorway. Watching. The street was deserted. A dusty worn out street with a two-bit pansy hood working a very sloppy tail. Unless it was meant to be obvious. I stood there watching him and wondering about something Silas Griffin had said that had surprised me. What was it? That Rhonda Park had told him about the murder?

127

She had surely tried to make us think the murder was news to her. Why?

'Mr Griffin,' I beckoned to him. 'Come here and take a look at this guy. Do you know him?'

Silas Griffin padded across the floor in his hush puppies and peered out the window. He reached into his pocket and took out a pair of Ben Franklin glasses and perched them on that pointy, red nose.

'No, I don't know him. Should I?'

'Not necessarily. He hangs around at the marina, a friend of Yaeger's.' Susie had gotten up and come to join us at the window. She looked down and was shaking her head. 'His name,' I said, 'is Quin Jefferson. He's dangerous – more psycho than not, I'd say. He tried to kill me with a knife last night and I threw him off the pier. On the whole, I'd guess he'd like to cut my heart out. I don't know how he's tied into what happened on your yacht, Griffin, but I got the feeling he is. Which makes him dangerous to you – '

'But why, for God's sake?'

'If for no other reason,' I said, 'than that he's following us and we came to you – '

Griffin look startled. 'Does that mean he followed you to see Rhonda? Damn it, have you put her in danger, too?'

'I don't think so. It was your boat, not hers, and so far as I know she's not involved in any equation with you and the Marina people.'

'But you can't be sure!' Griffin looked a trifle apoplectic. 'If anything happens to Rhonda – '

'Keep your shirt on or you'll have a stroke,' I said. 'I'm doing the best I can to keep your life taped together, which is a hell of a lot more than anyone else seems to be doing. I don't think Rhonda is in any danger but I'll go back and check. So try to keep cool – '

Susie interrupted, biting her nail: 'Do you think this Quin person is following us to find Daddy?' She cast an anxious glance at her father as if it were her responsibility to keep him safe from an unfair and cruel world.

'I don't know, Susie,' I said. 'But a guy like Quin is more or less capable of any craziness. Look, Griffin, take my advice and don't leave this loft for the next day or two, until you hear something from me. Have you got food to last?'

Griffin had begun to look scared. 'The freezer,' he muttered.

'Good. You just stay put and play with your computers and keep the door double-locked. You've got a bolt and a Yale. Just sit tight and don't open the door for anybody – '

'Rhonda – '

'You can look through the peephole, then.'

'Listen,' he croaked, cleared his nervous throat, and belted back some more Sprite. 'Why are they after me? What the hell have I done to anybody? I don't know anything about any of this, I was just living quietly here in Venice until you showed up and suddenly there are people with knives lurking outside wanting to kill me – what gives?'

'Nothing, I hope,' I said. 'Stay inside until you hear from me. And we're gonna get through this in one piece. It's just going to take a bit of doing.' I slapped him on the back and he didn't look too happy about the way things were going. Susie looked worried, too. I couldn't really blame them. The thought of Quin Jefferson and his knife wasn't doing my tummy much good.

But when we went back downstairs there was no sign of him.

My lucky day.

Chapter Seventeen

I had the feeling that trouble was creeping up on me. It was seeing Jefferson, sure, but it was also that little extra sense you develop when you've worked enough cases and watched them lie there twitching, blinking, tongues darting out, just before they strike and chew your face off. I'd found out a lot of things on the way to locating Silas Griffin and they were bound to fit into some kind of pattern. Maybe Silas Griffin actually fit into that pattern. Maybe not. He said he was an innocent bystander and I found him pretty persuasive. The absent-minded scientist with a new girlfriend, trying to straighten himself out and get a faltering career back on the road, confounded by a wife who hadn't worked out and a son who was pretty determinedly going his own way. And little Susie who loved her Daddy and somehow felt responsible for him.

And Silas Griffin owned that damned yacht. What had happened to his particular *Baja Dream*, anyway? Somebody got killed on it and some hot icons got left behind. And the stiff had had an affair with Susie. And the wife had known about the affair but Silas hadn't. And Rhonda Park said she didn't know about the murder but Silas said she told him about it . . .

And the yacht was tied up at the marina run by a gay pal of the son with whom he might have run some drugs . . . on another guy's boat. And there was the guy with a knife who wanted to spear me like a cock-tail weenie.

It was like trying to make a pattern out of too many pieces. But I'd wound up back at the guy with the knife and that made me think about the trouble creeping up on me. It was time to go it alone.

I walked Susie back to the pile of junk with a wheel at each corner and told her I wanted her to drive it back to San Amaro for me. Right away.

'But why? Why aren't you coming?' She was confused and I didn't blame her. She was cute when she was puzzled. She got a cute wrinkle across her forehead and her lower lip pouted and she looked about four.

'I want to check out a couple of things down here, no big deal,' I said. 'But Quin Jefferson and his knife might turn up again and that's five miles of bad road you don't need to walk. That's between him and me. And the fact is, I want to know why he's following me. I don't believe it's just because he's pissed off. There's a real reason and it might tie this whole thing together . . . because he's not doing it on his own. He's the kind of guy who does what he's told. I want to know who's telling him.'

'And you don't want me in the way – '

'I don't want you to get hurt.'

'You really are sort of brave, aren't you?'

'If it makes you feel better to think so, I'm a knight in shining armour. Just take my car and go home. I'll be in touch – '

She leaned up on tippy-toe and kissed me. Such are the rewards of being mistaken for a brave man.

She got into the car and noticed the cracked wind-shield and the general state of disrepair, which as a passenger she'd ignored. I handed her the key and she gingerly got it started. I assured her it ran more or less properly. 'Think how lucky you are,' I said. 'When you're driving it, you don't have to look at it.'

I watched her head off down the empty street which had the look that only a beachfront town can have. And I looked up at the warehouse loft and felt slightly reassured by Griffin's willingness to hole up for a while.

Bart had told me he was an egomaniac, all the monograms and whatnot, but he hadn't struck me as all that nuts. Maybe the starch had been taken out of him, as Rhonda had put it. He'd had to face quite a lot of his life coming apart, and the loss of economic well-being in the face of the kids making it so big must have been a bitter dose of reality. But it might have been the making of the inner man, if that was a consolation. He may have been forced back on his own resources and discovered what was really important. If he had, then it had been worth it, whatever the price. I was beginning to feel so righteous and wholesome I was making myself sick.

I walked back to Rhonda Park's apartment and she was just pulling up in a shiny little Toyota. The afternoon was gone and the cool ocean breeze was noticeable, wisps of fog just barely visible, like very shy ghosts.

'How did the audition go?' I asked.

'Icky. I'll never get it.' She was carrying a sack of groceries and I took them from her.

'Maybe you just don't look constipated,' I suggested.

That took her by surprise and she burst out laughing. 'I guess that's one of the nicest things anyone's ever said to me,' she said, shaking her head. 'I thought I'd heard them all but that's a new and improved line. You've earned yourself a drink, Professor.'

I followed her in to her place and she built a couple gin and tonics, sliced limes, and we sat on her little deck which jutted out from the side of the building. Clouds were rolling in off the water and it was getting dark fast.

'So, what's the scoop on Silas and his daughter?'

'They had a nice reunion. And I scared hell out of him. Now he thinks somebody is trying to kill him – '

'Is someone?'

'Beats me. He's the genesis of this case for me. It all swirls around my looking for him. I'm curious, though – why did you lie about not knowing of the murder on his yacht? He said you're the one who told him about it.'

She watched me over the rim of her glass, made a circle of the top with her finger.

'I don't know.'

'That's it?' I asked after the silence grew a little oppressive.

'You asked me a question and I said I didn't know the answer. When in doubt, shut up. Didn't Lincoln say something about that? Better to keep your mouth shut and let people think you a fool than open it and leave no doubt.'

Pretty good advice. Sounded like something Susie would wear on a tee-shirt. 'So, you just don't know why you lied?'

'You got it.'

'Are you going to see Silas tonight?'

'You said he's locked in and has his orders – '

'He'd see you – '

'Well, no, I'm not, actually. I've got a script to read

134

for an audition tomorrow – not a commercial, either. It's for a soap. An aerobics instructor!' She laughed.

'Typecasting,' I said. 'You've got the body for it.'

She nodded and sipped her drink. 'Why don't you stay for dinner? We'll just throw something on the grill – '

'What about your script?'

'You could go over my lines with me. Cue me.' She was grinning.

'What primitive humour you have, my dear.'

She let out that spontaneous laugh again.

We had another drink and I managed to mind my manners and avoid her clever actress's traps. I called her a temptress and a brazen hussy and she laughed and finally I left, ready to fight any foe and bear any burden in the defence of American womanhood.

Which was about the time I began to feel tired and stupid and wished to hell I had a car so I could just get the hell out of Venice and leave Silas and Rhonda and all the rest of them to work out their own problems. But my car was tucked away in San Amaro and I'd seen the bus station earlier in the afternoon when we'd arrived.

I walked back past the loft and looked up at the light in the windows and figured that I really hadn't had to stay behind when I sent Susie home. But, still, I felt better. Silas was safe and Rhonda was safe and I'd done what I had to do. All their doors were locked and they'd been alerted and there wasn't much more I could do. The danger, after all, probably existed only in my own mind.

The streets were even more deserted in the darkness of evening, if that was possible, and the fog was blowing more thickly. There's nothing like the smell of the ocean embedded in the fog.

I was getting chilly so I decided to cut through an alleyway leading back toward the main drag where I'd seen the bus station.

I was scuffing along, hands in my pockets, rocks in my head, whistling a happy tune, when a tiny sound in the darkness caught my ear.

And then, in the dim glow of the streetlamp at the far end of the alleyway, a man stepped out in front of me.

'Oh, for Christ's sake,' I said.

It was Quin Jefferson, accompanied by his knife.

His eyes were like pinpoints of fire, as if he were a special effect, lit from within just to scare the likes of me. His face had a blank, passionless look to it, as if he were mechanised, programmed by his own nuttiness to do a job, revenge his lost honour.

'You're a dead man,' he said.

'Oh, come on, Quin. What's the point of this? I'm just a guy trying to do a job for a friend – look, I'm out of it, I found the girl's father, everything's fine. Let's just let bygones be bygones.'

He stared at me. He was younger and far more fit than I, so running was out of the question. Getting past him in the alleyway was a hopeless folly.

'Listen, Quin, I've got a gun. I'd hate to shoot a homicidal queer, but if you force me – '

He responded to the insult much as one had hoped he might. He came at me fast, telegraphing everything he was going to do. All I had to do was leap nimbly to one side and deliver a deadening karate chop as he passed by.

Veal chops with a side of spaghetti carbonara I know. Karate chops, no. Nureyev I'm not. I fell down while trying to leap nimbly aside. My manoeuvre took

136

him by surprise and in the course of executing a leopard-like quick stop and turn he became tangled up in my feet. As I struggled to stand back up, he fell down with a grunt.

I kicked out, trying to free myself, and hit his face. He tried to push my foot and leg away and I tried to get up to run the hell to daylight. I heard my trousers rip, felt the knife blade sliding along my bare leg. His arm, it seemed, was trapped within my trouser leg. The sensation was doubtless like watching a centipede crawl up your leg under the sheet.

I did a little dance trying to get away and get my gun out. He managed to cut his way out of my pants, still blocking my way. He was on his feet in a flash and we stood face to face. Only one of us was out of breath.

Then he came at me again. Honest to God, I didn't want to shoot him. So I stepped out of the way again and laid a forearm across his face. He staggered backward. It's enough to make you think the guy with the knife is at a disadvantage. I hit him again with the forearm and then rushed him, slamming him up against the brick wall at the side of the alley. I twisted his arm and banged it against the wall a few times like they do on television and he dropped the knife. He squirmed away and I tackled him, forgetting for the moment that I had no idea what I'd do with him if I succeeded in making him stay put. I was pushing his face into the ground and he was spitting out dirt and I couldn't get my breath.

'You . . . killed . . . Sanchez,' I gasped.

'No, no, not . . . me – '

I pushed harder.

'Man,' he struggled with the words, 'I . . . can't talk like this – '

'You killed him – '

'No, no way – '

'Then who did?'

'Jesus, let me up . . . I'll tell you, you're . . . breaking my . . . bloody neck . . .'

I figured maybe I was. I loosened up a bit and he slowly got up on one elbow, then sat up. He saw I was now holding a gun on him. 'Stand up,' I said. 'And please, don't make me shoot you.'

He nodded, still wheezing, and stood up.

'Now who killed Sanchez?'

He never got the chance to answer.

I heard the flat crack of the shot from the darkness at the end of the alley, from where I'd come. There was a muzzle flash from the blackness and I felt Quin Jefferson jerk and slide past me on his way to the floor of the alley he'd so recently vacated, and I got off an answering shot at the flash. A second, two seconds, and it was all over. I went toward the dark end of the alley but there was no one there, not even the sound of running feet. Your head doesn't really work all that clearly at such moments, that's the thing. I was still hearing the two gunshots, mine and the killer's, and I don't know if I could have heard the sounds of anyone getting away. In any case, there was nothing to see and several minutes had passed and when I got back to Quin Jefferson there was still a little flutter in the eyelids and I bent down over him and asked him if he could hear me, asked him to give me the name of the killer who'd started with Freddie Sanchez and had now doubled his score. The eyelids fluttered, the lips trembled, and then he was gone. He'd been one nasty piece of work but now he was dead and defence-less and not much to worry about. Just a genetic mistake who'd gotten pretty much what was coming to him.

Somebody must have heard the shots and I didn't

know how much time had passed but I heard the sound of a siren coming closer. I figured the last thing I needed was the irritating formalities of a murder investigation. So I headed back down the alley, tried to wipe my sweaty face with my handkerchief, dusted myself off, tried to pretend that I always wore my trousers fetchingly split up the side, and went to the bus station. The northbound number was just about to leave and I bought my ticket and climbed aboard, sank into the comforting darkness. From my window seat I watched the patrol car with its flashing light pull to a stop near the bright end of the alley and two cops get out. They didn't know why they were there yet nor what they'd find if they poked around in the alley. They just had a report on some loud noises. Probably an old lady scared by a truck backfiring . . .

Chapter Eighteen

You want hot? I'll give you hot. Mexico City was hot. I've never been in Mexico City when it wasn't blinding and hot though I'm sure there are such times. I've flown all over Mexico at one time or another, in airplanes that made my VW look like a Maserati, in airplanes that would rather have just driven to the next town to hell with the flying part of it, and I have been sick in each and everyone of those parts of Mexico. I've been hot and sick from the water used to make the ice cubes. I've been sick from the food I found irresistible at a street vendor's emporium. I have been sick from tequila. Just from looking at the worm in the bottom of the bottle. I have been sick in Mexico. I have never gotten a social disease in Mexico, however, and that's nice. On the other hand, I've never really gotten lucky in Mexico, which may explain it.

On the other hand, I have never been sick in San Amaro.

Once I'd arrived back on the bus I gave my pants the once over, decided I'd been lucky not to get arrested for vagrancy, and threw them away. Such is the life of a big spender. I bathed, read a note left by Jan in which she expressed a certain ill-concealed irritation at not knowing my whereabouts. The name of Susan-Your-Student was tossed about with abandon. She wondered where Susan and I had run off to, which was not like her, leaving a preposition at the end of an angry question. I was too tired to call her. I kept reliving my fight with Quin Jefferson but in the replays I was losing. Then he was getting shot and I was blazing away at the darkness. I took some ancient sleeping pills and went to the arms of Morpheus, as they say at the madhouse, trying to plan what I'd do next.

Why next?

Because I had the feeling that maybe the killing wasn't over.

Which brought me to waking up with the idea that I'd better go to Mexico. Thank God I'm incredibly rich because this thing was now starting to cost me some real money.

Fool.

Hot.

The plane belonged to an airline which shall remain nameless, since they'd probably send gunsels to get me if they read this – the plane was hot and crowded and the airport at Mexico City was hotter and more crowded and I could feel my guts starting to send up panicky little cries of surrender. I couldn't stay long because I could neither drink nor eat. What a way to make a living. Except I wasn't making a living since no one was paying me.

However, I was hot on the trail of a murderer.

Well, not actually *hot*. But I was on the trail.

The Museum was long and low and some kind of very modern piece of statuary – looking as if it had been spun off of an Aztec model by a guy working in very up to date motifs, whatever that means – blocked the way to the entry so you had to go around it, casting admiring glances. Fountains splashed in the courtyard and the palms made huge splashes of shade and the receptionist in the office section buzzed Pablo Juzgar's office and told him I was waiting to see him. She listened and smiled at me reassuringly from obsidian eyes and told me that he'd see me as soon as possible, fifteen minutes to half an hour.

I wandered off and checked out some of the works of art and started yawning. I went out into the courtyard and sat on a bench under a palm and played guessing games with myself about icons and Sanchez and Quin Jefferson and the *Baja Dream* and drug smuggling and Tod Yaeger. The girls sunning in the courtyard were dark and gorgeous and they weren't sweating. I couldn't understand it. I was soaked. I was also thirsty. Time was running out. Soon I'd have to have a drink. A guy with a knife was more inviting.

Suddenly an enormous shape loomed out of the shadows at the other end of the courtyard, past the girls I was watching.

I knew it. Even though it wasn't wearing a dress.

Aaron Withers.

He stood blinking in the sunlight like a gigantic tortoise. His bald dome shone like a beacon. He was smoking a cigar the size of a ballbat. He wore his favourite colour, pastel green, a leisure suit by Omar the Tentmaker. A family of wetbacks could have used it for a house. He stood peering at several birds of bright plumage flickering in and out of the sun and shade, then slowly made his way along the path toward me. He passed within ten feet of where I sat. He didn't notice me or recognise me, anyway. He just waddled on his way, a symphony in green, like a watermelon with legs.

What was he doing so far south?

142

I kept thinking about those icons in his Malibu house.

Then the receptionist appeared at the doorway into the glass walled gallery and beckoned to me.

'My dear Professor,' Juzgar said. He was wearing a caramel coloured suit which fit him like syrup on a sundae, a cream shirt with a long collar and a pale blue silk tie with a matching square in his breast pocket. He gave his skinny gold wristwatch a quick look as we shook hands, just to show me that he was just as busy as ever. 'To what do I owe this most pleasant surprise?' He motioned me into a deep chair and sat down behind his desk. He lit a cigarette with his gold lighter and the gold ring winked at me from his little finger. It must have taken him hours to get gussied up each day.

'There was another murder back home last night,' I said. 'Someone who might be connected with the business of the icons . . . if, in fact, there was anything fishy going on with the icons and Sanchez.'

'Shocking,' he said. 'Who was killed, if I may ask?'

'Just a psycho punk. It's not who that's important but why – and we don't know why yet. Somebody shot him. He died in my arms. Which isn't as sad as it sounds. He was trying to kill me – '

'Good heavens! What's the world coming to, eh? It's all so hard to believe, that Frederico Sanchez should be involved in matters so violent.' He passed a manicured hand over his eyes as if he might be able to wipe the cruel world away. When he looked I was still there. He sighed.

'What have you learned about Sanchez and the icons?'

He squirmed in his chair and tapped the cigarette

143

ash into a cut glass ashtray. He rearranged a row of coloured pens on his blotter. He looked out the window of his office into the courtyard where the bright birds fluttered. Finally he had to say something.

'This isn't easy . . .'

'So I see,' I said. 'Murder never is, when you stop to look at it closely. You can't really make it pretty.'

'Ah, no. Well, much as I hate to admit it – after all, the man had been my colleague for many years – our investigation here leads me to the conclusion that Sanchez may well have been responsible for the thefts. We've conducted interviews with the staff and Mr Sanchez had asked a series of fairly incriminating questions about the icons . . . and for that matter several other kinds of art, paintings and sculpture. Not, I must say, incriminating at the time he asked them – merely curious. But in light of his murder and the discovery of the three icons with his body – well, then, very incriminating. The result is that we're going to have to have a look at every small piece in the collections he spent time researching – a laborious task, I'm afraid. It could be months before we know how much might have been stolen over the years. Assuming for the moment that he was guilty of long term theft, the loss could be substantial. And terribly difficult to determine accurately.' His shoulders heaved in a mighty shrug and he smoothed back his already slicked down grey hair. 'In short, we have a mess on our hands. I'm still hopeful that we can keep the lid on it, publicity-wise, at least minimizing it. It's a sorry truth that there are many unscrupulous collectors willing to pay fabulous sums for certain items.' He sighed again, apparently at the inexplicable duplicity of his fellow man.

'Unscrupulous collectors,' I repeated. 'Like the

man who just left here, would you say? Aaron Withers? He doesn't seem absolutely steeped in scruples.'

'I don't understand. You are acquainted with Aaron Withers?'

'In a manner of speaking. His name has come up in the course of this investigation – '

'Aaron? You must be joking – '

'Let's pretend I'm dead serious. I visited Withers in his home the other day and guess what I saw – '

'I can't imagine.' He was going a little frosty on me.

'He's got a house full of icons. You can imagine my surprise.'

He frowned at me as if I'd made a rude noise or used a four letter word in front of his wife and daughters.

'May I say that Mr Aaron Withers is a very old, very good, very personal friend of mine?'

'It's okay with me. I'm not responsible for your taste in friends.' I smiled.

'He is a well-known collector.'

'Of what? Hot icons?'

'He came here to renew our friendship and to console me on the loss of Mr Sanchez – '

'So Withers knew Sanchez?'

'Inevitably, I suppose they met. I may even have introduced them. Here, probably, at some museum function – hardly anything suspicious. Now, perhaps we can conclude this.' He looked at the watch again and stood up. 'I have many appointments – '

'Only fitting for such an important man,' I said. 'But I want you to know that I think Aaron Withers was buying the icons Freddie Sanchez stole from this museum. Which doesn't say much for you or the quality of your security. Unless of course you were involved – '

'Professor! I must insist – '

'Just a joke, Juzgar. Where's your sense of humour, man?'

'No, no, no.' Juzgar was shaking that smooth dark head. He looked like a cannon shell wearing a suit. 'Aside from the absurdity of your accusation about me, I can assure you that Mr Aaron Withers would never deal with a thief. He is above reproach. A very wealthy man – '

'Ha! What's that got to do with it? The biggest crooks in the world are the richest – '

'A man of immaculate manners. And reputation.'

'Are you sure we're talking about the same guy? Big fat character? Likes pastel greens? Wears a dress sometimes?'

Juzgar closed his eyes at the vulgar ruffian who was despoiling the hallowed halls of his museum and, in particular, his office. He might have been doing a slow burn in a silent movie.

'Mr Aaron Withers might conceivably purchase a stolen painting, something minor, with a false provenance . . . but it is simply inconceivable that he would ever deal directly with someone of the criminal classes. The man has . . . class. Surely, you must be able to see that . . .'

'Must be two different guys,' I said. I left him standing importantly behind his large important desk wondering what the hell my game was.

Chapter Nineteen

I got back into my rented car which had been resting in the sun. You could have roasted a turkey in the front seat. I opened the windows and turned on the air conditioner and stood beside it for a while and wondered if Juzgar might have been in on the Sanchez scam. Hell, Juzgar could have been the thief, selling to Withers or someone else, and Sanchez could have found out about it, tracked them to San Amaro and gotten killed for his trouble. I sort of liked that one.

But they wouldn't have left the three icons behind. Would they? Maybe they didn't know the icons were there . . . But if they'd been buying or selling them they must have known. Unless Sanchez had, unbeknownst to them, intercepted a shipment which would make him an icon hijacker, of which there must be comparatively few in the known universe . . .

Or maybe the heat and the lack of water was getting to me.

Or look at it from another angle. Maybe Withers was in it with Tod and Bart and Quin, and Sanchez was doing the stealing and . . . and . . .

It was definitely the heat.

I decided to go find my fat friend.

It wasn't tough.

I tried the Hilton first and he'd checked in that morning. I called his room and he was able to restrain his joy at hearing from me. I asked him if he'd like to come down and buy me a drink since he was so goddamn rich.

He told me to go wait for him in the lanai by the pool. I wandered out and found a bamboo stool beside a bamboo bar beneath a thatched roof. The bartender looked like Pancho Villa and the waitress looked like Lupe Velez. I looked like hell because I was remembering the chance I was taking if I had a drink.

'How about a Perrier? A cold one. No ice.'

'Perrier on ice,' he said.

'No. Just a cold one.' I was still explaining what I wanted when Withers came rolling up. He had exchanged his pastel green jacket for a mammoth safari shirt with more pockets than a pool table. It flapped outside his slacks. A bunch of cigars stuck up from one breast pocket like sticks of dynamite. He was puffing on one as he reached the bar. He ordered a glass of wine, thereby solving the problem I'd been confronting with one simple stroke. French wine. He turned to me, tried to asphyxiate me with one exhalation, and pursed his thick lips.

'Come clean, my man. Have you been following me?'

'No challenge in that. I could see you a mile away.'

'Well then, what's the meaning of this?'

'I'm sort of half-heartedly trying to pin a murder rap on you – '

'You'll have to try harder than that, I'm afraid.' He sipped his dark crimson wine and gazed calmly out at the pretty girls lolling about the pool. 'We're speaking of the late Mr Sanchez, I assume?'

'He'd do. And if I can't get you for murder maybe

the receiving stolen property rap will fit. We'll find something.'

'I very much doubt it. But press on, if you must.'

'How long have you known Rhonda Park?'

He laughed loudly, his chins rolling like a rough sea. 'Rhonda what? I've never heard of her. But you are having a go, aren't you? Rhonda . . .' He kept laughing. 'Try me again.'

'What were you doing down in Venice last night?' I tried to keep a very straight, very serious face. 'No point in lying. You were seen.'

'Balderdash, my man. I was home. Playing darts with several friends. They'll testify to that effect.' His eyes narrowed and all but disappeared in the pudding of his face. 'Venice,' he mused. 'I understand that someone was murdered last night in Venice. You couldn't possibly have reference to that?'

'How did you hear about that?'

'Read it in the *Los Angeles Times* this morning. Sorry to disappoint you. Young fella found shot down in an alley.'

'Funny you should make the connection to my question – not that you're not a mighty sharp fella yourself.'

'Not so funny, really, Professor. I take it that you didn't see the paper this morning?'

'No I didn't.'

'Then I have a question for you – if you didn't see the papers how did you know someone was murdered?' He began to laugh again, like an explosion deep in a cave.

'None of your goddamn business,' I said defensively. This wasn't going quite the way I'd planned. 'I still want to know why you connected that with my question about your being in Venice last night – '

'Simple. The story said that the murder victim was

149

employed at the San Amaro Marina. It wass something short of genius to think that there might just possibly be a connection to the Sanchez matter.' He sighed heavily and drained off his glass of wine. 'You know, you're a nice enough chap, Professor. But you're really not . . . *much*. D'ya see what I mean? Not a heavyweight.'

I looked him up and down.

'Nobody gonna say that about you,' I observed.

I had to hand it to him, though. That big booming laugh followed me all the way across the lanai as I walked away trying to maintain the last tattered shreds of my dignity.

Chapter Twenty

I caught a morning plane back to Los Angeles, and when I boarded I noticed that Aaron Withers, daintily turned out this morning in sky blue, was taking up most of the first class section. He filled two seats with the armrests removed and two first class seats is a lot of seats. I wondered if he had to buy two tickets. I supposed he didn't give a damn one way or the other.

I scrunched into my own tiny chair, fought off the hunger from having eaten as little as humanly possible (toast and a Coke for breakfast seemed safe), and stared out the window at the low white clouds that looked solid from above, like we could land on them in an emergency.

Had my trip to Mexico made things any clearer? Or had I just been spinning my wheels?

Sanchez was the thief, that looked ninety-five percent certain. Withers was a real collector: that is, it wasn't just an assumption of mine, anymore. Juzgar tied Withers to Sanchez – at least they had him in common. That was one triangle.

Then there was Sanchez, the *Baja Dream*, and the Marina.

That tied Sanchez to Yaeger and Quin Jefferson. Another triangle.

Withers had kept tabs on Bart Griffin and Bart Griffin was tied to Yaeger and Silas Griffin.

So much for triangles. I was getting into squares and who knew what lay ahead? Trapezoids and rhomboids? The sky was the limit.

But somewhere in all the welter of information, disinformation, lies, half-truths, and sheer confusion, a single comment – since this is a mystery story, there's always the telltale comment – was leering at me, ducking away before I could quite recognise it. But it was there. A lie that would bring the whole structure of lies the killer had created come tumbling down.

What the hell was it?

I slept a bit and dreamed of Susie Griffin and her fetish for older men and in my dream I was one of them and when I grabbed her tee-shirt the quotation came apart in my hands and I was holding her tight and she was running her tongue across her lips, beckoning me on, and she told me she was mad about me, and the bad thing was I knew she was lying. She was a liar and she was dangerous and I couldn't stay away from her, although I knew I was making a hell of a mistake.

Fine thing when a man can't even enjoy his dreams. After all, that's all it was. Just a dream of a thirsty man. When I woke up I was smiling and the stewardess was telling me to fasten my seat belt.

It was foggy and damp in LA and after I ransomed my car from a level on a far side of the San Andreas Fault, I noticed that the Serenade in Blue waddled directly into a waiting Mercedes sedan while the voice on the loudspeaker kept warning people that if they parked there they'd be submerged at one in one of the LaBrea Tarpits. Like all those old dinosaurs. Withers didn't give a shit what the voice said. I figured I had the guy down pat. He just did what he damn well pleased and figured somebody would come along to clean up the mess. I'm sure he was almost always right.

I drove north and the fog was like cotton wool. It took forever. Everything came looming at you at the last second and I was a nervous wreck by the time I got the VW back into San Amaro and down the sandy streets to the beachfront where I lived.

Jan was standing in the doorway by the time I shut off the ignition. There was no sneaking up on anyone with the VW. It can't be done. It's like having a siren attached to the top of the car, only the VW makes more noise.

Jan was wearing jeans and an Irish fishing sweater and loafers with no socks, and her honey tan and blonde hair streaky from the sun made me want to commit a crime right there in the doorway. But she was waving to me as I walked toward her and the surf was raising hell just behind the house and I couldn't hear a word she was saying. But it didn't look like the love call of a Californian girl eager to mate.

I grabbed her and kissed her, ignoring her bleats of protestation, but the squirming didn't stop. Something was out of whack and I leaned back and asked her if all this was any way to greet her man back from foreign parts.

'Will you please act like a human being for a minute!'

'Why start now? I'm much too old to turn over a new – '

'This is serious, you fool!'

'Took you long enough to notice – '

'It's Sue Griffin! She's been trying to reach you all morning and where the hell have you been? I was up all night calling hospitals and psycho wards – '

'I'd swear I left you a note somewhere – '

'So where have you been?'

'Mexico City.' I told her what I'd been doing and she poured me a cup of coffee and I begged her to throw together an onion and cheese omelette, with a Clark bar on the side.

'Don't they have food in Mexico?' she muttered.

'It's a long and ugly story, me and food in Mexico. So what does Sue Griffin want?'

She was breaking eggs and whisking them and chopping onions and slicing cheese and I knew that this was the woman for the rest of my life. I was that hungry. While she was talking I went to the fridge and drank a Dr Pepper. I'm talking thirsty, man.

'That's just it – she doesn't know if anything is wrong or not. But she was pretty upset the last time she called. She's been calling her father's place in Venice and nobody answers. And she says you told him not to go out for a few days, until you told him it was okay, and he promised he wouldn't – is this all true? Where do you get off telling people things like that?'

'Oh, Jeez . . . this is pretty complicated, Jan. I'll fill you in. First, I better call the kid.' She brought the omelette and the toast and the blueberry jam and more coffee and gritted her teeth when she put the ketchup bottle down before me.

She poured her own cup of coffee and sat down opposite me. 'She said she called some friend of his, a Rhoda or Rhonda Something, but what's important is this woman hasn't seen him either. Who's Rhoda?'

'Rhonda. She's old man Griffin's girlfriend.' I chewed solemnly, deliberately, joyfully. 'This is wonderful,' I said.

Jan looked at me as if I were insane.

'Well, I don't believe it,' I said. 'Can she have lost him again, so soon after I found him?'

'Sort of looks like it.'

I called Sue and she was flustered and sounded worried and didn't want to waste time on the phone. She didn't sound so much like a little girl. More like a worried woman.

'I know my father. He promised you he wouldn't go out – '

'Look, it's two days since then. Maybe he got fed up.' I didn't want to tell her I didn't think she had a clue about what sort of man her father was. Maybe daughters never do. Too much hero worship. Something like that. Wish I had a daughter . . .

I told her I'd be right there.

When I put the phone down I felt Jan's eyes boring into the back of my head.

'This time, Buster, I'm going along, too. No more of your little trips with the college girl!'

I called my dean at the college and held my nose and told him I had the flu and could barely speak, let alone lecture.

He was a smart guy. He said he believed me. But he didn't. That's how you get to be dean, I suppose.

Chapter Twenty-one

I don't mind dying.
I just don't want to be there when it happens.
                                    – Woody Allen

She was wearing a sweatshirt over tight white jeans and the lettering was in white. I'd have felt better if the quotation hadn't dealt with death. Her face, for the first time since I'd known her, had lost its freshness. Today it looked pinched, dark around her eyes, and her makeup had been sloppily applied, leaving a streak across one cheek.

I introduced her to Jan and she got in back. It was the sort of day I sort of wished the top worked. The fog hadn't gotten much better and there was a nip in the air. A mile of driving along the ocean would have frozen a brass monkey. In the event, I would have to do.

We stopped for coffee and to warm up. Wrapping both hands around the cup, Susie told us why she'd been calling her father.

'It's important,' she said. 'I mean, I might have called him anyway just to see how he was holding up in his forced confinement – but the thing is I've been talking to Shirley and I told her about him, how he seems to have straightened out his drinking and gotten back to work . . . and Shirley just upped and said she thought maybe it was time the two of them got together to talk about a reconciliation! Can you believe it!' She tried to look hopeful but I doubted if she thought the idea made any more sense than I did.

'It's a little hard to believe,' I admitted. 'Did you tell her about Rhonda?'

Susie nodded. 'More or less. I mean, I didn't make a big thing of it – '

'But it seems to me it is a big thing,' I said.

'Well, the way I see it, it's up to Shirley and Dad. I'm not going to butt in.'

Before we left the roadside joint I told them about what happened in Venice after Susie drove my car home. They sat there with profoundly disbelieving looks on their faces while I told them of Quin Jefferson dying in my arms and my taking a shot at the killer.

'But who killed him?' Susie asked.

'How should I know?'

'You are the detective,' Jan reminded me.

'Well, I don't know. Susie, I keep wondering where your brother Bart figures in all this. If anywhere. Did he know Quin Jefferson?'

'I don't know. If Tod Yaeger knew Jefferson, I suppose Bart might have. Bart didn't talk about his friends much.'

'Okay,' I said. 'We might as well get this finished.'

It hadn't gotten any warmer in the poor old VW.

Venice was shrouded in the same fog I'd spent the whole day battling my way through. It was a little colder in Venice and the streets were a little more deserted. The beach looked like Mars, with a single skater weaving soundlessly along the path. I turned off the main street after passing the bus depot and the alleyway where Quin Jefferson had died. There was a chain of police department sawhorses across the mouth of the alley and a couple of uniformed cops standing guard.

The street looked even more desolate without the sunshine. I kept thinking that maybe Silas Griffin had gotten a little stir crazy and gone out for a while, figuring I probably didn't know what the hell I was talking about.

I parked across the street from the loft building. The lights were still burning. Susie looked up expectantly and I got out.

There was somebody coming down the stairway from the second floor, blurred and indistinct because of the fog.

I ran across the street.

'Hey,' I shouted, my words losing their way in the fog. 'Hey, hold on there! Who is it? You – '

He turned and walked toward me.

Susie and Jan reached my side.

'Bart!' It was Susie who recognised him first and then he came into sharper focus, looking just the same as he had when I'd met him. Uninvolved but civil enough. 'What are you doing here?'

'What would I be doing here, Sis? Coming to see Dad. What's the big deal?' He turned to me. 'Hi, what's happening? I see you found the old man okay.'

I introduced Jan and asked him how his father was.

He shrugged. 'Beats me. He's not home. I thought he might be wrapped up in his gear, not listening, so I knocked for a while and called his name . . . y'know, with the lights being on and all, I thought he might be in there. No dice. He must be out. Door's locked.'

I started up the stairway.

'It's no use, man,' he said. 'It's locked.'

'I don't doubt you for a minute,' I said.

They all followed me up and stood in anticipation while I tried the door.

'Told you, man.'

'Okay, Bart, we're going to have to get this door open. As I recall it's double-locked. Fairly heavy oak door.' I looked at it like a man sizing up a bear. 'We can't get much of a run at it up here.' It looked like maybe four feet max. Jan and Susie were standing a couple of steps down the stairs.

'We're gonna need a crowbar. But Dad's gonna be real mad when he comes back – '

'I'll handle that,' I said. 'We've got to make sure he's all right. You got a crowbar in your trunk for changing tyres?'

He did. So did I.

When we got to work on the door it was fairly slow going. It fit tightly. So we wedged and banged and grunted and swore and thought about how easy it always is to break open doors on television. We were both dripping wet and Susie was almost beside herself by the time we were nearing the end of the job.

I could hear the locks pulling loose inside, the splintering of the wood and the doorframe and the screeching of the nails heating up as they were forced through the wood. Finally it was open, only an inch or so but we were able to push it back. It twisted on its hinges.

The lamps in the far end of the room were burning and the place hadn't changed. It wasn't messed up, there hadn't been a struggle.

At the working end of the loft his stacks of gear and screens and wires were all in order. No violence had been done to anything. The drawing board was standing upright.

No violence had been done to anything . . . except Silas Griffin.

He sat in his drawing chair, slumped forward over the table.

When she saw him, Susie let out a little whimper and went closer and stopped when she saw or smelled the blood.

Bart's face went white. 'Christ . . .'

Jan put her arm around Susie's shoulders and held her tight.

I went over to the dead man and lifted him up. The front of his shirt was all wet and the stain looked thick and black. He'd lost a lot of blood before he called it a lifetime. It looked to me like he'd been shot once in the chest and died where he sat. I leaned him back in the chair and Jan took Susie to the couch where she'd sat two days before. Bart looked at his father for a long time, shaking his head, then went to sit beside Susie. He took her hand in both of his and didn't say a word. Eventually Susie rested her head on Bart's shoulder. She had lost a father but maybe she'd gained a brother. I hoped so.

I told them what had happened even though everybody knew he was dead. I just wanted to make it official. Jan went to the fridge and got everybody something to drink. I went back to Silas Griffin.

He had lived long enough to scrawl something on the paper on his drawing table. I looked at it and blinked. For a moment I couldn't believe it.

Icon.

What had he been trying to tell us? *Icon.* Everywhere I turned in the case I ran into the bloody damned icons.

Behind me I heard Susie crying softly. Bart hugged her and she buried her face against his plaid flannel shirt.

I crooked a finger at Jan and she came to me and I

pointed at the scrawl and told her what she didn't know about the significance of the word.

'What does it tell you?' she asked.

'You always ask the worst questions. I'm thinking. Something will come to me. He must have had some involvement with the icons . . . but what?' I felt a headache coming on. 'Icons on his boat. Dead man who stole icons on his boat. Now he's dead and his last thoughts are of the icons. Don't worry, it'll come to me.'

Jan made a tour of the room and turned back to me triumphantly. 'All the windows are locked from the inside,' she said. 'The door was double locked. It's a locked room murder!'

Susie began sobbing again, then wiped her tears and smiled sorrowfully at Bart.

'Not quite,' I said.

'And why not?' Jan replied. 'It absolutely is – '

'No. He *could* have lived long enough to shut and lock the door after the murderer left, presumably to prevent his sudden return. After all, he did live long enough to write the word *Icon* on his drawing paper – '

'You don't *know* he wrote it after he was shot. He may have been writing it and was interrupted and shot and died instantly and then the killer escaped leaving a locked room!'

I had to admit she had me there. It was possible. Though how he could have gotten out baffled me.

Bart spoke up. 'Could it have been suicide?'

'No way,' I said. 'There'd have to be a gun at hand – and there's no powder burns – '

'I don't understand,' Susie said. She was fighting back the tears, biting her thumbnail. 'You told him he mustn't let anyone in and he promised you he'd do as you said. He even said he had food in the freezer. Why would he suddenly let someone in?'

I didn't much like the implications of her question.

'There's only one reason that I can think of,' I said. 'It had to be someone very close to him, someone he loved, someone he had no reason to regard as a danger . . . There aren't many people who fit that description. You're one, Susie. But you drove back to San Amaro . . .'

'And I was either with Shirley at the house or with the girls where I live.' She wasn't providing an alibi. She was thinking out loud.

'Doesn't leave many alternatives,' I said.

Chapter Twenty-two

The Venice police were taking their time interviewing each of us. They'd done me first and then I'd gotten permission from the scene of the crime people to make some coffee. I'd called Phil Redding even before calling the locals and Jan and I were sitting on stools at the kitchen counter drinking hot black coffee when I heard his heavy step on the stairway. He came in looking bleary-eyed and smoking a corncob pipe with tobacco that smelled like burned chocolate. He came over to us, said hello, and went to clear himself with the Venice homicide people. That took a while and a bit of ribbing to establish what damned good fellows they all were, and then Phil came back to me and I handed him a cup of coffee.

'You look terrible,' I said.

'Goddamn Rotary breakfast this morning. Couldn't sleep all night. Worst thing I've ever had to do . . . I hadda coupla belts at lunch just to help me forget – '

'What's so bad about a Rotary breakfast?' Jan asked.

'Mayor Gonzer. It was in his honour.' He sipped at the scalding coffee. 'Some jerk picked me to give the big speech. It was humiliating.' He rubbed his eyes. He looked around the loft, took in the body which he'd already inspected with the Venice guys and looked at Bart and Susie talking to a cop. 'So what the hell's going on here, anyway? Can't you stay away from murder? You used up a lifetime supply already . . .' He sighed and puffed on the pipe and drank his coffee and sighed and groaned as I told him the story of finding Silas Griffin's corpse.

'There's some real obvious stuff,' he grumbled. 'Oughta be easy to figure it out – '

'Too much obvious stuff,' I said. 'The hard part is to figure out what to discard as irrelevant.'

'Just cut the Sherlock Holmes bit, Professor.' He gave me a sour look and I laughed. 'First, we got Sanchez dead on Griffin's boat. Second, we got Griffin dead. Now that could be – could be – a coincidence, though damned unlikely. But this dying word on the drawing table . . . *Icon* . . . that locks up the connection, in my book. Three icons with Sanchez, *Icon* the last thing Griffin tells us. If I were as smart as you think you are, I'd be able to solve it with that much – '

'But you're not and neither is Matt,' Jan said. 'Now don't quarrel. Be good boys and be constructive.'

'He's been dead a while, Phil,' I said. 'A day or so, anyway. That means the killer came to see him after I told him to sit tight and not let anyone in until I called him and gave him the go-ahead – '

Phil choked on some smoke, sputtered a moment or two, and jabbed the pipestem into my chest. 'What in the name of God are you talking about? Since when do you inform the citizenry to take cover? Come clean, chummy – what have you gotten into you haven't told your betters about?'

'It's a little weird,' I said lamely. 'I was going to tell you – '

'And so you are, my fine friend. Right now.'

'Well, you heard what happened to Quin Jefferson – '

'Another marina rat. Yeah, I know what happened to

164

him. The inevitable. What's that got to do with you?'

'It happened down here in Venice – '

'I know that, Professor. Let's start on the stuff I don't know.'

'I was there. I'd had a run in with him at the marina and he wound up in the water. He didn't like it, told me he was going to kill me. I didn't think much more about it. I found Silas Griffin for Susie and we came down here to visit him a couple of days ago. We were sitting around up here shootin' the breeze, I happened to look out of the window, and who should I see loitering in the street keeping an eye on this building? None other than my friend Quin Jefferson. Now either he was going to a hell of a lot of trouble to follow me just to stick a knife in my guts . . . or he had followed us to find Griffin. Maybe he was keeping an eye on Griffin and didn't have to follow us to find him. Either way, he was watching me or Griffin. Now, why would he be watching Griffin? Nothing came to mind immediately so I did a little cogitating – '

'Here comes the Sherlock Holmes bit,' Redding groused.

'Not really. I just tried to think of a reason. And I thought maybe Jefferson and Yaeger had been using the *Baja Dream* for their meetings with Sanchez – maybe they were fencing the icons and anything else Sanchez could smuggle out, maybe other pieces of art, maybe drugs, anything. And if Jefferson and Yaeger were up to no good with Sanchez on Griffin's boat, then Griffin might have found out about it. That would have made Griffin doubly dangerous to Jefferson and Yaeger – he knew they were fencing stolen goods and that they'd killed Sanchez . . .'

Redding gave me an appraising look. 'That is without doubt one of the iffiest theories I've ever heard!'

165

'I didn't say it was exactly airtight,' I said.

Jan said: 'Don't forget we've got a locked room here – '

'Oh, no, not that!' Redding groaned. 'I hate those!'

'Well, it *is* locked,' she insisted.

'He must have let somebody in,' Redding said through clenched teeth, 'since he didn't kill himself! Please, Jan, give me some kind of break – '

'I don't see why I should.' Jan has a lot of bulldog in her.

'Would Griffin have let Jefferson in?' Redding had decided he didn't have the guts to argue with her. Smart guy, in his way. Took me a long time to learn.

'I can't see him letting either Jefferson or Yaeger in,' I said. 'He hated Yaeger on a variety of grounds, including the trouble Bart and Yaeger got into. Unless . . . no, that's not – '

'Unless what? Give! Come on – ' Redding's fuse wasn't getting any longer.

'I don't know. Unless Silas Griffin was in partnership with Yaeger and they were both keeping it secret, hiding it behind an open enmity.' I shrugged.

'Whew,' Redding sighed. 'That's beautiful. Of course, Jan here *may* have been in on it and having a wild affair with Sanchez and Griffin and done them both in . . . Christ, Professor, get serious!'

'Just a thought. You gotta think of everything when you can't make all the pieces fit.'

'Well, back to reality.' Redding was making notes on a pad. 'Griffin opened his door to someone. He wasn't shot close up, in the doorway, because there'd be powder burns on his shirt. No . . . he must have gone back to his drawing board and then the killer fired. Or maybe Griffin was just standing by the board – we can't tell. Anyway, the killer thought he was dead and left . . . but Griffin was still alive. There's the bloody handkerchief on the floor that he used to try to slow the bleeding. He managed to get back to the door and lock it, then back to the drawing table, trying to rest before he called for help . . . but he was losing blood and the weakness hit him like a building falling on him. So he decided he'd leave a clue of some kind and the clue is that one word . . . *Icon*. We just don't know what the hell the clue is supposed to mean . . . hell, it's supposed to name the killer or something.' He threw up his hands in frustration.

He looked at me.

'Don't look at me,' I said.

Jan said: 'You'd better tell him the rest of your Quin Jefferson story.'

Redding looked at me expectantly.

'Ah,' I said. 'Well, later that night I was getting ready to leave Venice and he jumped me in an alley – '

'The night he got killed? Jesus, Professor!'

'We fought in an alley, he had his knife, he was pretty damn serious. But miracles never cease – I had him down, I got my gun on him – '

'You still got a licence for that thing?'

'Obviously,' I said. 'I had him right on the verge of telling me who killed Sanchez – '

'You mean he said he knew?'

'Yeah. He was just gonna tell me when, bang, a shot from the dark at the end of the alley got him. I returned fire but the killer got away and I was left with Jefferson's body. I got the hell out – '

'And didn't report it to anyone until now,' Redding glared at me.

'Okay, okay, I was going to.'

'You really should be in jail,' he muttered.

'Don't be so picky,' I said. 'It's unbecoming.'

'My ass,' he said, frowning at me.

Chapter Twenty-three

Later that night the police were through with our statements and Redding had already headed back to San Amaro. Bart decided to follow us back and Susie went with him. Jan fought off the desire to ride in an enclosed vehicle and bundled up to come with me in the VW. For some unknown reason the heater worked, which kept our legs warm while the rest of us got a quick fix of pneumonia. I was sneezing by the time we got back to San Amaro. Susie had asked me to go back to the big house with her and Bart. She wanted somebody else to break the news of Silas's death to Shirley. Susie was still in pretty rotten shape. When we left the cars in the big forecourt she was red-eyed and sniffling and Bart was wearing a stoic face.

Shirley had already gone to bed. She came down in her robe and the news hit her fairly hard. She didn't sob or yell and scream, but she got very quiet and left the drink fixing to me and put her arm around Susie, who curled up with her on the couch, crying softly. Bart was already acting a little like the man of the house, comforting both of them and making a couple of calls to Griffin's lawyer and a funeral director, alerting him to the situation. It was interesting watching the kid start measuring up, as if all he'd needed was the opportunity. Which came, unfortunately, with the death of his father.

When Jan and I finally left them I had the feeling they were in pretty good hands.

The next morning Phil Redding called me. Jan and I were still in bed. My nose was stuffed up, my throat was sore, and I started sneezing as soon as I woke up. Jan looked at me and, having lived through my colds before, covered her eyes and said, 'Oh no, please God, not one of his colds . . .'

She got up and began rummaging in the medicine cabinet for leftover Contacs and cough medicine and a Nostrilla nasal spray which turned out to be empty. All I really wanted was a couple of mugs of hot chocolate.

Phil said I sounded funny and I asked him to tell me what in the name of God he wanted at this unseemly hour.

'It's almost noon,' he said.

'What do you want?' I pleaded.

'I've spent the morning grilling Tod Yaeger. He says he doesn't know a damn thing about any murder, Sanchez's or Jefferson's or Griffin's. None of them seem to concern him much, either. He acted like Jefferson was just a stray dog who got ran over on the highway. Nice fella, Mr Yaeger.'

'Do you think he could kill somebody?'

'Damn right. And eat a hearty lunch right afterward.'

'Anything else?'

'You got a cold or what?'

'Goodbye, Phil.'

'Yeah, there is something else. I called Pablo Juzgar in Mexico City. He's getting a little tired of this but

169

I laid a bunch of stuff on him about the possibility of something far more widespread than we'd thought, told him we had another murder tied in with the icons . . . anyway, I scared him into coming back up here to "aid us with our investigations." He's coming in this afternoon.'

Jan arrived with a Contac, a tablespoon and the cough syrup, a glass of orange juice, and the empty nasal spray. I took the Contac with the orange juice and a double dose of cough syrup. I felt worse right away.

'You still there?' Phil asked.

'Well, at least Juzgar and Withers are in the clear as far as the Griffin killing. I was with them in Mexico City when Silas was getting killed – '

'Think again. The ME in Venice says Griffin died up to forty-eight hours before you found him. Which means he could have been killed the same night Jefferson got killed – which means the same guy probably killed them both, one after the other. The bullet lodged near his heart and the ME says he couldn't have lived too long after he was shot – maybe an hour, maybe a good bit less.'

'So nobody's in the clear,' I said.

'That's the way it looks to me. Withers could have done it before he went to Mexico City and right now all we have for the time of Juzgar's flight back to Mexico City is his word. He was in a hell of a hurry that day . . . maybe he was in a hurry to kill a couple guys. He could have taken a different flight or even a private plane. It is, my lad, in the words of Yul Brynner, a puzzlement.'

Phil kept talking but my fevered mind, punctuated by the occasional sneeze, was working its way back through the corridors of memory.

Something had dropped into place and the whole piece of machinery was beginning to purr.

I remembered something that someone had told me – something that couldn't possibly be true. A lie. A lie which made no sense coming from an innocent person! But only from a murderer . . .

'When will Juzgar be here?'

'Like I said, this afternoon. You paying attention, Professor?'

'I'm thinking and sneezing. You can't expect me to pay attention, too. Can you do yourself a big favour, flatfoot?'

'Such as?'

'Get all these bozos together out at Shirley Griffin's house tonight. All of them – can you manage that?'

'Oh, I wouldn't be surprised. A man who can sell his soul and give a speech in honour of Mayor Gonzer can do damned near anything!'

It was another cool night and the fire was roaring in the fireplace. I stationed myself as near it as possible. Jan was nearby with all the necessary supplies for the unmasking of a murderer. A huge box of man-sized Kleenexes. A fresh container of Contac. A bottle of Tylenol. A new bottle of cough syrup. A Nostrilla nasal spray and a Sinex to fall back on. Armed with these various materials a first rate detective can scale any heights. Unfortunately, in this case, he also kept sneezing.

Shirley Griffin was there in a long plaid skirt and a white silk blouse, no boyfriends in attendance, nary a muscle builder. She was holding a tumbler of scotch. I wanted one myself but Jan had thrown a fit, informing me that scotch mixed with all the medicine I had in me was bound to launch me into the Pacific.

171

Seemed to me a good idea but she prevailed because I felt weak and feverish.

Bart was on hand, almost unrecognisable in a blue blazer and grey slacks and polished loafers. He shook my hand when I arrived and blessed me when I sneezed and almost blew out a picture window. Susie was not wearing a cute quotation and looked tired and withdrawn, though she kissed my cheek. Jan told her she shouldn't do that again unless she wanted my cold. Oh, that Jan!

Tod Yaeger sat by himself in a deep chair, staring with some curiosity at Bart who must have presented him with a side of his personality Tod hadn't seen before. Tod looked like a man who wanted to get out as quickly as possible but didn't want to miss the fun.

Pablo Juzgar hovered elegantly near Shirley Griffin and Susie, flicking his little gold lighter and looking at his skinny gold watch. Susie, unless my eyes deceived me, cast an occasional covert glance his way. After all, he was an attractive and older man. But she was having trouble working up much enthusiasm.

Aaron Withers was a veritable cloudbank of coffee coloured leisure suit, smoking a giant cigar, filling most of a loveseat, his stubby legs out in front of him and crossed at the ankles. He seemed marvellously unconcerned but, then, that was his style.

Rhonda Park had chosen Withers to spend time talking to. She'd perched perkily on the arm of his chair but she wasn't smiling. From what I could hear, she wanted to know if this little get-together was official or what? Withers grinned like a buddha and told her he thought it might turn out to be fairly serious business before it was over.

Phil Redding called for their attention.

'Let's get to this,' he said gruffly, 'before the Professor here expires and we've got another stiff on

172

our hands. He asked me to invite you all here tonight and I figured why the hell not? This is a complex case. Or series of cases. And he seems to think he can unravel things. Professor, it's all yours.'

I sneezed several times, all in the name of making an impressive entrance.

Bart blessed me.

'Look, everybody,' I said. 'I now know . . .' I began to cough.

Tod Yaeger laughed. A shrill sound.

Juzgar grumbled.

'I now know who killed . . . uh, everybody that's been killed.' Sniff, sniff.

'Knowing it,' Aaron Withers said, 'and proving it are two very different things, Professor.'

'How true,' I said. 'Fortunately for me, I not only know it. I can prove it . . .'

I grabbed for the Kleenex and blew my nose.

Nothing's ever easy.

WHO KILLED FREDDIE SANCHEZ? QUIN JEFFERSON? SILAS GRIFFIN?

WHAT WAS THE MOTIVE?

HOW DID THE KILLER GAIN ACCESS TO GRIFFIN'S LOCKED ROOM?

WHAT WAS GRIFFIN TRYING TO TELL THEM WITH 'ICON'?

WHAT WAS THE LIE THAT THE PROFESSOR REMEMBERED AND WHICH POINTED THE FINGER OF GUILT AT THAT PERSON?

HOW CAN THE PROFESSOR PROVE THAT HIS SOLUTION IS THE CORRECT ONE?